A
CRY OF
PLAYERS

A
CRY OF
PLAYERS

A PLAY BY

WILLIAM GIBSON

ATHENEUM *NEW YORK*

for
TOM & DAN
and all the young who will not obey what is

A CRY OF PLAYERS was first presented by the Berkshire Theatre Festival, Stockbridge, Massachusetts, July 24, 1968, with the following cast of principals:

WILL	*Frank Langella*
FULK	*Michael Egan*
MEG	*Lois Kibbee*
RICHARDS	*Robert Donley*
SUSANNA	*Jackie Paris*
ANNE	*Anne Bancroft*
KEMP	*Dan Morgan*
SIR THOMAS	*William Roerick*
NED	*Peter Galman*
BERRY	*Brendan Fay*
SANDELLS	*Bill Moor*
ROCHE	*Ray Stewart*
JENNY	*Flora Elkins*
HODGES	*Jerome Dempsey*
HEMING	*Tom Sawyer*
ARTHUR	*Terrence Hall*
OLD JOHN	*Don McHenry*
GILBERT	*Jess Osuna*

It was then presented by the Repertory Theatre of Lincoln Center, New York City, November 14, 1968, with the following changes in cast:

MEG	*Rosetta LeNoire*
RICHARDS	*Ray Fry*
KEMP	*Robert Symonds*
NED	*Rene Auberjonois*
POPE	*Gerry Black*

ARTHUR	*Kristoffer Tabori*
SIR THOMAS	*Stephen Elliott*
JENNY	*Susan Tyrrell*
GILBERT	*Ronald Weyand*

Both productions were directed by Gene Frankel.

Production Note

THE STAGE *is almost bare, except for some arrangement of a rear platform which serves variously; a single decor piece—a tree, a stocks, a casement window, a banister—helps to identify each locale, and may remain simultaneously in sight here and there, or not.*

THE LOOK AND SOUND *of the play must not be stage-Elizabethan. The people in it have not yet discovered the fork, they live in filth, and wear rags not unlike those of, say, Appalachia; their songs are crossed by the rhythms of our time.*

ACT ONE

ACT TWO

ACT THREE

The action occurs in an obscure town in
England, one autumn in the 1580's.

ACT I

———

I would there were no age between sixteen and three-and-twenty, or that youth would sleep out the rest; for there is nothing in the between but getting wenches with child, wronging the ancientry, stealing, fighting.

SCENE 1

MOONLIGHT ON PLATFORM; A TREE. THREE SURREPTITIOUS
VOICES APPROACH, WHISPERING AND SINGING.

VOICES [OFF]:
>　　*'Twas I that paid for all things,*
>　　*'Twas others drank the wine;*
>　　*I cannot now recall things—*

(WILL, *a tipsy youth in leathery work-clothes,
climbs into the moonlight.*)

WILL: Full moon. Milady, brimful in the high places,
what are we for?

(FULK *climbs tipsily on, middle-aged, filthy, one-
armed; he has a wine jug.* MEG, *equally filthy, follows with fish on a pole.* WILL *reaches for the jug.*)

Fulk, wine is a thief.
FULK: Dry as a stick, boy.
MEG: *Falero! lero! loo!*

FULK [HISSING]: Shut up, ye old bag, ye want the game-
keeper on us?

(*They listen, not moving.*)

WILL: What use I'm to make of this shell of its former
self brings me to the pith of the evening.

(*He retires with the jug to urinate into it;* FULK
sits to cut the fish from the pole.)

FULK: Let's divide the forbidden fruit.
MEG: What fruit?
FULK: The fish. Now there's four smelly fish—
WILL [APART]: And three smelly poachers—
MEG: Speak for yeself, boy.
FULK: Hey, ye scholar, how many times does four fish
go into three poachers?
WILL: Once into, once out of—What's that?

(*They listen, not moving.*)

FULK: Is it the keeper, is it the keeper?

(*An arrow springs into the tree at* WILL's *hand,
quivering.*)

WILL: Flee for life and honor!

(*They scatter;* RICHARDS *comes running in with a
crossbow.*)

RICHARDS: Stop there! Stop or—Ye hear me? Stop!

(MEG *reappears, running.*)

MEG: The fish, the fish!

(*She grabs up the pole;* RICHARDS *tackles her.*)

RICHARDS: Got ye! Ha, poaching fish, are ye?
MEG: Let me go, let me go—
RICHARDS: Stealing the fish, see what Sir Thomas says—
MEG [WAILS]: Let me go, there's plenty fish left—

(WILL *and* FULK *running back in yank at* RICHARDS'
feet, and hoist him by the ankles.)

WILL: Run, you lubber cow!
RICHARDS: Put me down, ye thieves, put me down!
FULK: Down?
WILL: Down!

(THEY *drop* RICHARDS, WILL *thrusts the jug into his
hands, and* THEY *run out.* RICHARDS *holds the jug
with its last gurgle over his face, and is outraged.*)

RICHARDS: Piss? Ye murdering thieves, I'll get ye—

WILL, FULK, MEG [OFF]:

>   'Twas I that beat the bush,
>   The bird to others flew—

RICHARDS: I'll see ye in the stocks yet!

(The singing fades, the moonlight dies; the drum
of the following scene is heard at once.)

SCENE 2

MORNING; AN EMPTY STOCKS. A DRUM AND A TRUMPET,
DISTANT, APPROACH WITH A STIR OF VOICES; A YOUNG
CHILD, SUSANNA, RUNS IN.

SUSANNA: Mamma, Mamma!

> (ANNE, *a comely woman of 30, enters bearing a washbasket.*)

Mamma, the players, they're coming!
ANNE: What, love?
SUSANNA: The players, Mamma!

> (*Ragged* TOWNSPEOPLE *gather onstage, in a crescendo of excitement.*)

TOWNSMAN: Is it the players?
TOWNSWOMAN: They say it's players coming to town—
TOWNSWOMAN: Are they coming here, are ye sure they're coming here?
TOWNSMAN: Listen, ye can hear them—

TOWNSWOMAN: Will they be acting us plays, d'ye think?

TOWNSWOMAN: Why else are they coming? It's players all right—

SUSANNA: Can I see the plays, Mamma, can I, can I?

ANNE: And why not, won't we all see them, ye little goose?

TOWNSMAN: Listen to them! Can ye see them coming there?

TOWNSWOMAN: It's Kemp, it's Willie Kemp and his men!

(*The procession of* PLAYERS *spills onstage, surrounded by a clamor of* TOWNSPEOPLE, *unkempt and brutish. The* PLAYERS *are led by little* KEMP, *skipping and beating a drum; the others are* NED, HEMING, POPE, *and a boy,* ARTHUR, *all carrying bundles.* KEMP *leaps upon the stocks, instantly the showman.*)

KEMP: Good people of this good town, new faces and old friends, I say old friends because I've been here before. Who remembers proud, handsome, lordly Kemp?

ANNE: I remember ye, Willie Kemp, poor man, ye haven't grown an inch—

KEMP: And I remember you, that honest face looking up at me in admiration, just before you threw the turnip. Friends, is there any of you believes in plays?

(*Cheers.*)

And will you come to see our plays?

(*Cheers.*)

I'm glad to hear you. We see some men with black suits and behinds like pins would take the bread out of the mouths of players, they say plays teach lewdness. Do I look like a lewd man, I won't give you time to answer that, but beware or the black suits will take away all your sins. Now we'll be here three days, plays every afternoon in the inn-yard, old favorites and a new play never—

(SIR THOMAS, *a tall and austere man with a stick, enters with* RICHARDS; *the crowd becomes chilled.*)

SIR THOMAS: What is the purpose of this gathering?
NED: Why, we're players, sir.
SIR THOMAS: Players. Come to distract our people from their work, and show them lies, and take their pennies with you.
KEMP: We don't show lies, we show fables, to take their minds off themselves—
SIR THOMAS: Let them think on themselves, and their actions as creatures made in the image of God. Allegedly. Berry!

(BERRY, *a hulk of a man, pushes through the crowd.*)

BERRY: Here, sir.

SIR THOMAS: Must I myself keep the streets clear? Vagabonds may be whipped out of town, and they know it.

NED [ANNOYED]: We're not vagabonds, sir, we're players in service.

SIR THOMAS: You are attached to a peer?

KEMP: Show the paper, Ned.

(NED *passes a paper to* SIR THOMAS, *who reads it.*)

SIR THOMAS: The Earl of Leicester is a great man: he should know the parable of the blind leading the blind. You are not licensed to gather in the square. Acquaint yourselves with the proper procedure, and follow it.

KEMP: The people were here. We thought a word to them—

SIR THOMAS: Berry, take these jugglers to the Gild Hall. The bailiff will license you to perform in the inn-yard.

BERRY: Clear the street, clear the street.

(He *shoves the* TOWNSPEOPLE, *who begin to disperse.* SIR THOMAS *turns to leave as* WILL, *in workclothes filthy with blood and muck, runs in; he collides with* SIR THOMAS, *who stares.*)

WILL: I'm sorry. Will Kemp!

(SIR THOMAS *brushes his sleeve off, and goes;* BERRY *pushes* WILL *aside,* WILL *pushes back.*)

BERRY: What?

WILL: Why do you push at me?

BERRY: Because I'm to clear the crowd out of—

WILL: I'm not the crowd, the others are, push at the others. Kemp!

ANNE: Oh, God help us, I'll push at ye—

(*She captures* WILL, *buttons his shirt up. The* PLAYERS *start off.*)

Run around naked as a baby's bottom, God knows what's in ye head, cabbage worms?

WILL: Kemp!

KEMP: Eh?

(WILL *tosses an apple,* KEMP *catches it.*)

WILL: Polished it with my own spit, for old times.

KEMP [SCOWLS]: What old times?

WILL: An apple orchard—

ANNE [BUTTONING]: What are ye doing here at all? Gilbert's off in—

WILL [BREAKS FREE]: —you and a fellow felon, twelve years old, if you remember?

KEMP: No.

WILL: Please remember me—

(*But* KEMP *is gone, pulled by the others.* SUSANNA *runs to* WILL; SANDELLS, *a big and dogged man, is watching.*)

ANNE: Why aren't ye in the valley with Gilbert?

(WILL *stands moveless, unhappy, with* SUSANNA *at his leg.*)

WILL: I was.
ANNE: Was? Is that what—
WILL: I saw Kemp and his men, I ran to catch them.
SUSANNA: I saw them too, Papa, I saw them too!
WILL [SWINGS HER]: I saw you see them too—
ANNE: Oh Will, put her down! I don't know which of the two of ye is the child. If ye left Gilbert to finish the kill—
KEMP [BACK IN]: Orchard, orchard! Why, you little skimble—
ANNE [MEANWHILE]: —he'll come home black as rain, I can't always be—
KEMP: —skamble apple thief, you've grown up!
ANNE: —fighting him off ye—
WILL: Yes, yes, and you too, but not up.
KEMP: Jigging, wears away the legs. But I didn't forget the apples—
WILL: Nor I you. Or whose orchard it was?
KEMP: Whose?
ANNE: Will!

WILL: In a moment. His eminence, this injustice of
the peace.

KEMP: Sir Thomas?

(*They begin to laugh.*)

ANNE [HARD]: I was talking to ye.

(WILL *comes back, quick, winsome, low with her.*)

WILL: Anne, let me have a word with him, it's a difference of two worthless to everyone but precious to
me minutes, and I'll run all the way to Gilbert for
his pardon that I enjoyed them.

ANNE: Oh God, ye're a busy lad for doing nothing.

(*She waves him back.*)

KEMP: Let's do it again to him.

WILL: We will. Not apples, venison this time?

KEMP: Oh, venison any time. And you remembered
me, now that's—

WILL: You and a glimpse of something—great men,
deeds, passions—

KEMP: Oh, the plays.

WILL: —the kingdom of what we are and never become: how could I not remember you while I
lived?

KEMP: Believes in plays! It puts a lump in my throat,
which calls for ale—

WILL: Oh, I—

KEMP: Come.

WILL: No, the—cupboard is bare, I must—

KEMP: I meant I'd buy you a pot.

WILL [TORN]: I wish I—My brother is—

>   (*A deep breath.*)

>   —but later, and it was a pleasure.

>   (*He delivers* SUSANNA *to* ANNE.)

Done.

ANNE: Here.

>   (*She finds a coin in her pocket.*)

Don't look so sickly, pet, ye can have one ale with the man, now don't be all day.

>   (WILL *hesitates, takes the coin, blows a kiss to* ANNE, *and rejoins* KEMP.)

KEMP: Friend of yours, you dog?

WILL: No.

KEMP: Mother?

WILL. Wife.

>   (*They go off.*)

ANNE: Mother! Are ye blind, ye little dwarf? (*She glowers after them;* SANDELLS *approaches her.*)

SANDELLS: I'd box his ears.

ANNE: Who?

SANDELLS: Pays ye no mind like that, and the next thing ye give him money.

ANNE: Oh Sandy, will ye let me be? I get sick of hearing it. Give him time, it's only the boy in him and—

SANDELLS: Boy.

ANNE: —it cheers me to see it now and again.

(*She starts off with the washbasket.*)

SANDELLS: It cheers ye about the Hodges girl?

ANNE: What?

SANDELLS: I hear tongues wagging about him and the Hodges girl, I—thought ye knew—

(ANNE *stares;* SIR THOMAS *enters followed by old* ROCHE, *who carries a couple of books.*)

ROCHE: —the news of these players. Do you plan to attend, Sir Thomas?

SIR THOMAS: Certainly not.

ROCHE: Nor I. Ah, Anne! This is the wife. Sir Thomas is thinking of adding his recommendation to mine, Anne.

ANNE: Recommendation for what?

ROCHE: Why, Redditch.

ANNE: Redditch?

ROCHE: Has the boy not told you?

SIR THOMAS: A vacancy there has come to my attention.

ROCHE: Teaching the school.

ANNE [WIDE-EYED]: Schoolmaster?

SIR THOMAS: Do I know the young man?

ROCHE: I did see him earlier—

ANNE: No, he's at work now.

SANDELLS: At work.

ANNE: For his father, helps his old father—

ROCHE: Yes, skinning and so on. But my ablest student
      in—

(RICHARDS *enters, unhappy*; SIR THOMAS *calls.*)

SIR THOMAS: Did you encounter them?

RICHARDS: No, sir. I'm not sure I'd—

SIR THOMAS: Richards, I will not be invaded by these
      louts.

ANNE: It's books he—

RICHARDS: I had my hands on one, sir, I was outnum-
      bered.

ROCHE: —my ablest student in more years here than
      I care to—

ANNE: He is a bright one, sir, everyone agrees to that,
      reads, writes, teaches our—

SIR THOMAS: I am not impressed by what everyone
      agrees to, and least by women. Would you know
      him again?

RICHARDS: Who, sir?

SIR THOMAS [PATIENTLY]: The one who outnumbered
   you.

RICHARDS: It was a her, I might know by the feel—

ANNE: We have three children, Sir Thomas. This is
   Susanna, bob to Sir Thomas, and twins at home
   not out of the cradle—

SIR THOMAS: Yes, yes. Bring him to me, Walter. Continue searching.

RICHARDS [HOPELESS]: Yes, sir.

(*He goes off one way;* SIR THOMAS *walks another.*)

ROCHE: We go the same way, shall I walk along with
   you, Sir Thomas?

SIR THOMAS: No.

(*He leaves.*)

ROCHE: A strange man. I shall stop in this evening,
   Anne, do ask Will to be at home?

ANNE: Yes, come early enough I'll—

ROCHE: And Anne. Sir Thomas likes a quiet woman.

ANNE: Does he, well, God put the tongue in my head
   and it wasn't for kissing anyone's behind with.
   I'll have him at home.

(ROCHE *pats her cheek, and goes;* ANNE *turns back
to* SANDELLS.)

Is it talk, or do ye—

(*She spies* SUSANNA *squatting.*)

Ye'd best run along, chick.

SUSANNA [COMES]: Would ye like a present?

ANNE: What is it?

SUSANNA: A beetle.

ANNE: Take him home for me, don't eat him, run.

(*She starts* SUSANNA *with a pat on her bottom, watches her off first.*)

—or do ye know it, did ye see them or what?

SANDELLS: No, how could I see—

ANNE: Then don't bring me the gabble of every old frump who's jealous of me. Bring me a piece of good news about him for a change.

SANDELLS: I don't hear any.

ANNE: Ye just heard some, he's wanted for this school teaching, so.

SANDELLS: He won't take it.

ANNE: Won't—

(WILL *enters unnoticed.*)

Sandy, why is it ye never once give him the benefit, not since the first—

SANDELLS: He's no good.

(WILL *halts; after a moment* ANNE *takes up the washbasket.*)

Can I help ye home?

ANNE [CURT]: No.

WILL: I'll help her home, thank you.

(SANDELLS *regards, then ignores him.*)

SANDELLS: Ask if he'll take it, ye'll see.

(*He nods to* ANNE, *goes out.*)

WILL: This aging suitor of yours must find it a—

ANNE: He's an old friend, ye're not to make—

WILL: Whatever he is, tell him to keep his tongue off
me. If these folk so dislike the taste of me why do
they chew on me over and over, like cows?—down
into one stomach, indigestible, up again as cud,
chewed on, down into another, up, down—

ANNE: Nobody gives ye a thought.

WILL: —and when I come to the end of their pious
bowels, out of a remnant cowflop I could make
men with more wit than this old friend. I'm now
off to Gilbert.

ANNE: No, sit, Gilbert can wait.

WILL [STOPS]: Oh?

ANNE: Yes, I want a few words with ye.

(*She pats the stocks;* WILL *comes back to her,
guarded.*)

WILL: Well, I'm a man of few words—

ANNE: It seems a while since ye stayed put long enough
     to talk, let alone was near me, would there be any
     —reason for that?

WILL: A fevered imagination.

ANNE: Yours?

WILL: Yours. I talk incessantly.

ANNE: Not to me, lad, ye didn't even greet me on the
     street when ye saw me, but—

WILL: I didn't see you, Anne.

ANNE: Well, if ye didn't see me when ye saw me it's
     worse, but it's not what I'm wanting to say. I only
     mean of late ye're—different.

WILL: From whom, I hope?

ANNE: No, changed.

WILL: Since?

ANNE: Since the twins, or—Will, I'm not—

     (*She is not hasty enough,* WILL *rises to pace away;
     a couple of* TOWNSPEOPLE *cross and gawk.*)

     —saying what ye think I'm saying, I know how
     a woman gets when she's carrying—

WILL: What in God's name can I do about—

ANNE: —blown up like a windbag—

WILL: —a muscle that obeys nothing but its own wishes,
     scold it into upright behavior?

ANNE: I'm not talking about that now, will ye listen to
     me once, damn ye, Sir Thomas wants—

(*She spies the couple gawking, and glares at them.*)

How would ye like a basket of wet wash in ye eye?

(*They hurry out;* ANNE *averts her face, a hand at it.*)

WILL: Anne, you're not crying? I—
ANNE: No, I'm not crying! Every pair of jackass ears on the road has to know I'm ugly to ye—
WILL: This is what you're not talking about.
ANNE: I'm talking about the wild things ye do! Ye didn't use to, why is it now ye're here, there, flighty as a grasshopper—
WILL: Look, I try to ape what I see, this—round of sacred duties uses so little of me I could—

(*It bursts out of him.*)

—quarrel with the angels! What, is so much of us meant to rust and rot? I come into town any hour it seems to me like a charnel yard, peopled by cadavers, who each morning walk out on their master's errands and at night are called back to their—coffins.
ANNE: It's a grand view of house and home. Ye're so wretched?

WILL [A PAUSE]: Oh God, I don't know why, the sun is warm, the fruit hangs on the trees—

(*He weighs the apple in his hand.*)

—eat, drink, and be married. Here.
ANNE: No.
WILL: Apple. Do you good.
ANNE: I don't want to eat an apple now—
WILL: Please.

(ANNE *takes a first bite,* WILL *a second; he sits with her.*)

Anne, I'm not blind to what you are, even when I see out of—bad blood—
ANNE: Well, ye're a great nuisance, but man and wife is ups and downs, lad, like any road. It's better than the ditch.
WILL: Yes, I remember the ditch.
ANNE: And if I keep at ye—about the work, or being wild—
WILL: Wasn't too bad in the ditch. Ups and downs, I was never up but you were down, and vice—
ANNE: Don't.

(*She regards him, and he her; he kisses her on the mouth.*)

Why do ye do that, to mock me?

WILL: No, to say you're—not ugly to me, Anne, I love you and I do foolish things.

ANNE [CHEERED]: Yes, well, there was one or two before ye, like Adam.

WILL: And he did eat.

(*He lies back, head in her lap;* ANNE, *with his hand at her lips, bites hard into his palm.*)

Heyy!

ANNE: Ye're not ugly to me either. Is it bleeding?

WILL: Not very much.

ANNE: Next time. Will, it's only the good opinion of Sir Thomas I'm talking about. Because if everything in the town here is such that ye can't be content, then—

(*She waits;* WILL *is very still.*)

—we'll go away.

WILL: To where?

ANNE: To Redditch.

WILL: Now there's a metropolis.

ANNE: Love, why didn't ye tell me about teaching the school there?

WILL: Well, there's a worm in this apple.

ANNE: I didn't know enough to feel proud of ye till Master Roche spoke. And he'll sup with us about it, so be at home tonight.

WILL: Yes, where else?

ANNE: Wherever else ye were at bedtime last night, sweet, ye didn't say.

WILL: I was walking.

ANNE: And I didn't ask.

WILL: I take note.

ANNE: Because ye can't—keep someone by pulling, can ye? Well.

(*She stands.*)

It's happy news, I'm thankful for it, dear husband, and the twins are famished—

WILL: Do we know?

ANNE: Oh, I—

(*A* thumb *at her bosom.*)

—have a clock or two. It's like loving anyone, ye feel what they—

WILL: I meant this news, happy or not. I don't look forward to what I see in this wistful old man—a dry rot of habit, deference—

ANNE: Ye're a young man.

WILL: I have hopes of being an old one, and I'd—

ANNE: If ye're making anyone old it's me. Now listen to me. If ye're wretched here with the skinning and tanning, then so am I, because ye're—angry with me too and it's a part of what's wrong, chick, I know that. But ye'll be rid of it once and for all

there, it'll be books instead, and to be schoolmaster with—

WILL: Anne.

ANNE: —people bowing to ye in the town is not the
worst thing could happen to ye for a change. It's
a sizeable step up, and we'll have our own house
there, without the old ones underfoot wherever I
turn, and we—

WILL: Don't—

ANNE: —have children don't get all they need here,
sharing with—

WILL: Don't inundate me.

ANNE: I'm not—what did ye say?—

WILL: Drown me with reasons, I—

ANNE: —drowning ye, but I have to speak the truth,
ye're not a boy now, ye can't live—

WILL: Speak, I speak my guts out and can't speak the
truth: and truths come off your tongue as easy as
spittle.

ANNE: Thank ye, pet.

WILL: Introduced by a dry tear.

ANNE: What?

WILL: I mean your show of distress and forgiveness, is
it by chance it leads us into this happy news?

ANNE: Ye think I—Oh, ye devil, I don't come to anyone
alive with tears!

(*She is on her feet in outrage;* FULK *enters in the
wake of a* TOWNSWOMAN *crossing.*)

And that ye know me so long and so little is what
causes a few of them—

FULK: Will, my lad! Anne. Well, well.

(*He comes, jingling two coins.*)

Am I in ye way? No.

(*He sits, confidential.*)

I'm a bearer of welcome tidings, boy. I—

WILL: Fulk, go away.

FULK [TAKEN ABACK]: I just came.

ANNE: Ye're not needed here. If anywhere. I'll thank ye
to let him be.

FULK [RISING]: Glad to, I only wanted to share the luck
of last night, Meg sold the fish. A pleasant day to
ye.

(*He ambles away;* ANNE *stares.*)

ANNE: What fish do ye mean?

FULK: Eh?

(*He eyes* WILL.)

Oh. No fish at all, did I say—

ANNE: Was Will with ye last night?

FULK: No.

WILL: Yes.

ANNE: Ye said ye were walking.

FULK [BRIGHTLY]: Yes.

WILL: No.

FULK: My—memory isn't what it was—

ANNE: Poaching fish. And in Sir Thomas's park, oh,
ye're a clever lad.

FULK: Now who told ye a tale like—

ANNE: I heard them talking! The two of ye, wasn't it,
why didn't ye say when I asked?

WILL [CAREFULLY]: You didn't ask, if I may quote—

ANNE [REMEMBERING]: And with a woman. Who?

WILL: —you choose not to ask, because—

ANNE [SHARP]: Who was it, Fulk?

FULK: Why, only an old drab ye wouldn't—

ANNE [WHEELS]: Was it Jenny Hodges?

WILL: Oh, Christ.

(*He starts out.*)

ANNE: God help me, it's true.

WILL [TURNS]: Anne, I was not—

ANNE: And that's why ye can't, with me, all these
months—

WILL: I was not with a woman.

ANNE: Don't lie, don't—

WILL: It was Fulk's woman.

FULK: If ye call it a woman.

ANNE: —lie, both of ye, hang together like thieves, why
do I listen? Lied about being there, ye keep things
from me, same as lied about the teaching—

WILL: And if I said yes to the teaching, you then keep
to your half of this compact?

ANNE: What half, what are ye—

WILL: Not to ask into my—misdeeds, isn't that the
compact, a certain allowance of wild oats if I say
yes to the teaching? Because when I said no the
questions flew, like bees. Don't—indulge me, Anne,
I—

ANNE: Ye're insane.

WILL: No, you turn me loose with the left hand and
draw me in with the right, like a dutiful—

ANNE: Stop it, stop, it's all excuses, lies and—

WILL: —horse, to pull the family wagon—

ANNE: —excuses, ye don't answer the one question
that—

WILL: —which I do, in my way, but to—

ANNE [VEHEMENT]: Are ye laying with Jenny Hodges,
yes or no?

WILL [A SILENCE]: Ask her.

(*Presently* ANNE *goes to the washbasket; she half
drops it, the wet clothes spill, and she gathers
them; when she is ready to lift it again* WILL *is at
it to help, and she strikes him across the mouth.*)

ANNE: When I need ye help I ask for it, boy, give it
where it's needed.

(*She goes out with the basket.* WILL *sees at his
feet something not gathered and picks it up, a*

*small sock, which he sits with, and works his hand
into.)*

FULK: Don't be down, boy.

WILL [PRESENTLY]: It's only you? Go down after some
—underground stream, all I come to is mud, us
and our daily mud?

FULK: Come, we'll drink yer share of the fish.

(After a moment WILL *somersaults backwards,
comes up with a tart song.)*

WILL:

> If I had been hanged when I had been
>   married—

FULK [WITH HIM]:

> My torments had ended, though I had
>   miscarried;
> If I had been warned—

*(They go off, arm in arm. Lights out; the dark is
pierced by the howl which opens the next scene.)*

SCENE 3

A PATCH OF MOONLIGHT ON THE PLATFORM AT THE TREE;
THE WILD HOWL LIFTS AGAIN, AN ANIMAL IN PAIN.

RICHARDS RUNS IN WITH A KNIFE, PEERS, DROPS INTO THE
SHADOW, AND STABS TWICE; THE HOWL DIES. CROUCHING
TO PRY WITH HIS HANDS, HE HEARS FOOTSTEPS, TURNS
WITH THE KNIFE READY, WAITS.

RICHARDS: Oh. Good evening, sir.

(SIR THOMAS *comes into a patch of moonlight below, gazing out.*)

SIR THOMAS: A good evening in truth.

(RICHARDS *resumes work.*)

The moon is kindly, even the odor of the earth is
sweet now. Who would think it begets such a
welter of creatures and their griefs, Richards?

RICHARDS: Sir?

SIR THOMAS [SEES]: Ahh.

RICHARDS: It's out of its misery, sir.

SIR THOMAS: I ordered no traps set, these animals bring
to this woodland the grace of living flesh—

RICHARDS: It's not meant for animals.

SIR THOMAS: What then?

RICHARDS: Poachers. It's man traps I'm setting.

SIR THOMAS: Man traps. You know what this will do
to one?

RICHARDS: Ye want these poachers, don't ye?

SIR THOMAS: Not served in their blood, thus.

RICHARDS: Ye'd put them in the stocks if ye caught
them—

SIR THOMAS: That is lawfulness, this is vindictive.

RICHARDS: I don't see the difference.

SIR THOMAS: It is the beauty of beasts that they are
creatures of instinct: the beauty of man is that he
is not. I shall punish our intruders, but this is
means tainted with their own fault.

RICHARDS: I want to pay them off.

SIR THOMAS: Yes. I have seen men for fifty years adoring
every master, however unfit: if passion and corruption are the shepherds, what should the sheep be?
Wenching, brawling, killing—

(*He toes the carcass.*)

How evil is his face.

RICHARDS: Can't hurt ye now.

SIR THOMAS: I meant death. It hurts most those whom
   it spares.

RICHARDS: It wasn't yesterday.

SIR THOMAS: What?

RICHARDS: That ye son was killed, and I don't see
   what—

SIR THOMAS: Remove these traps, Richards.

RICHARDS: Why? First ye ask me to catch them—

SIR THOMAS: So I do.

RICHARDS: —then ye ask me to don't, to—

SIR THOMAS: No, I ask myself which of the great, in
   this riotous land, will teach us to be simple and
   upright? In this town, I, at least.

(*He cleans his fingertips, gazing at the carcass,
then out again.*)

So comely by moonlight. Does it please God,
Richards, that it is the absence of true light makes
it so comely?

(RICHARDS *stares as* SIR THOMAS *goes off; he bends
to the trap, but ponders, turns on his knee to
mutter.*)

RICHARDS: No. Who'd they piss on, you?

(He *puts hands in pockets, and marches away. An outbreak of voices in song and laughter is heard, the moonlight dying on the tree as it rises opposite.*)

SCENE 4

A CASEMENT WINDOW, IN THE DARK; THE ROWDY VOICES
SINGING, SHOUTING, LAUGHING, ARE SPORADIC UNDER THE
ENTIRE SCENE.

VOICES [SINGING]:
> *Hey nonny no!*
> *Men are fools that wish to die!*
> *Is it not fine to dance and sing*
> *When the bells of death do ring?*
> *Is it not fine—*

1ST VOICE [SHOUTING]: Beer, Jenny!
2ND VOICE: Jenny!

> (*Moonlight now outside the window; a couple in*
> *an embrace on the floor*)

VOICES:
> *—to swim in wine*
> *And turn upon the toe*
> *And sing hey nonny no,*
> *When the winds blow and the seas flow?*
> *Hey nonny no!*

1ST & 2ND VOICES: Jenny, hey, Jenny!
JENNY [HALF OF THE COUPLE]: Coming, coming!

(*She kneels to button her bodice, an uddery girl.*)

Oh, ye get me in such—No, let go, ye can wait
till—
VOICES: Jenny!
JENNY: Coming! Ye'll be on the hill?
WILL [THE OTHER HALF]: No.
JENNY: Why?
WILL: I've reformed.
JENNY: Oh, have ye?
WILL [UNEAGER]: Yes, my—soul says flesh should be a
ladder up which soul climbs, wrong by wrong—

(*She lies on him in a long kiss.*)

Be on the hill. When?
JENNY: I changed my mind.

(*She rises; voices approach.*)

HODGES [OFF]: Ye can all work up here and no one'll
be in ye way—
JENNY: Oh, sweet Jesus—

(*Snatches up a tray.*)

—it's the old bitch himself—

WILL: Who?
JENNY: My father, hide—
WILL: Where? Isn't a mousehole.
JENNY [ZIGGING]: I—I—

(*She drops the tray, opens the casement.*)

Out the window, wait on the roof, hurry—

(WILL *comes; she resumes buttoning.*)

Oh God, I'm all hanging out—
WILL: You hide.

(*He helps her out the window onto the platform,
where she cowers and listens;* HODGES, *a sour character in an apron, appears with lit candles,* KEMP
following with three stools; lights up.)

HODGES: Who's that?
WILL: I, said cock—robin—
KEMP: There he is.
HODGES: What are ye doing up here?
WILL: Closing windows—

(*He shuts the casement, spies the tray.*)

—for the rehearsal.
KEMP: Innocent, you see.

(HODGES *looks around with the candles as* KEMP
sets the stools down; WILL *takes the tray to hide it.*)

This good man worries for his child—
HODGES [GLOOMY]: With reason.

(WILL *sits on the floor upon the tray as* HODGES
turns.)

What are ye sitting there for?
WILL: Sheer—fatigue—
HODGES [SETS THE CANDLES DOWN): What will ye drink,
    ale?
KEMP: Two ales.
WILL: One.
KEMP: Two.
HODGES: The boy's drunk already.
WILL: I'm not drunk and I—

(*He rises, but instantly sits on the tray.*)

—reconsider, three ales!
HODGES: Can't stand as it is.
VOICES [SHOUTING]: Jenny, Jenny, Jenny, Jenny, Jenny—
HODGES: Where the devil is that girl?

(*He steps outside, half in view, to call down.*)

Jenny!

(KEMP *throws some papers on a stool, sits to them.*)

KEMP: I didn't know we'd rehearse up here, how did
    you?
WILL: I'm—prophetic.
KEMP: Ho. Tell my future.
WILL: You will soon—admit me to a delicious re-
    hearsal—
KEMP [AT PAPERS]: I can't, lad. Ned won't have it.
WILL: I've been waiting, what else is of interest here?
HODGES [RECEDING]: Jenny?
WILL: If I thirst for your company—

(*He is up with the tray, passing behind* KEMP *to
open the casement.*)

—it's not for a mouthful of free ale.

(*He holds the tray outside.*)

HODGES [APPROACHING]: Jenny!
WILL: —which I might of course—

(JENNY *comes, takes the tray, starts in; he turns
her back.*)

—not now—
KEMP: Eh?
WILL: —but soon, repay—
KEMP: You will, if we go after the deer. Midnight?

WILL: Midnight, if I stay for the rehearsal.

KEMP [LOOKS]: What are you doing?

(HODGES *comes back;* WILL *stands against the window to block it.*)

WILL: Opening the window.

HODGES: I'll bring them myself. Three?

KEMP: One.

WILL: Two.

KEMP [EYES WILL IN SOME PERPLEXITY]: Two. It's chilly, would you close it?

WILL [UNMOVING]: Gladly.

KEMP: Well?

WILL: Gladly.

HODGES [EXASPERATED]: How many?

KEMP [LIKEWISE]: Two, two, two, one and one, half of four, five minus three—

(HODGES *retreats under his glare, off; at the window* JENNY *gesticulates at* WILL, *but he closes it on her, explaining.*)

WILL: It's chilly. Do I stay?

KEMP: Work on Ned. With my blessing.

(*He writes.* JENNY *marches around with the tray on her head, then sits, chin on hand;* WILL *looks over* KEMP's *shoulder.*)

Accounts.

WILL [POINTS]: One thirty-nine.

KEMP: What? Oh. You've a head for figures, drunk or not.

(*He sees* WILL'*s hand, wearing the sock.*)

What's that?

WILL: A beloved sock.

KEMP: I mean why do you think your sock is a glove?

WILL: Well, I could think my hand is a foot.

(*He sits, studies it.*)

I think it's a talisman, but I'm wrong, it—averts no evil the flesh is disposed to. See, this five-legged thing we dress in a—fabric of conscience, if you follow—

KEMP: Dimly.

WILL: —the question being, how should we live? be true to the flesh, this wrongdoer which is me, or to this fabric which is—others? I wear it to grope among these thorny questions, it's my child's.

KEMP: Older than you, isn't she.

WILL: My child? No.

KEMP: Wife.

WILL: Yes. Eight years.

KEMP: How did that happen?

WILL: My head for figures misled me.

(JENNY *opens the casement an inch to peer in as* HEMING *appears with a stool;* HODGES *follows with tankards.*)

Come in, come in, we're—

(JENNY *starts to come in.*)

No!

(JENNY *retreats in despair to the back of the platform.*)

HEMING: No what?
WILL: No—ale for me—
KEMP: Where's Ned?
HEMING: Arguing about the play.
KEMP: Who with now?
HEMING: The ostler. Says he laughs at the wrong places.
KEMP: Damn him, Ned convinces half of every town they've no right to enjoy the plays.

(*He accepts a tankard;* WILL *makes for the window.*)

HEMING [INDICATING]: Is he staying?
KEMP: Ned won't let him, even sober.
WILL: I'll ask Ned myself.

(ARTHUR *comes in with a stool,* POPE *tousling his hair,* NED *following with a stool.*)

POPE: —he's near the end of his female days, his voice is growing hair in its cracks. Did you hear him drop an octave in your love scene today?

NED: I heard him, and was not amused.

ARTHUR: I can't help it.

JENNY [GASPS]: Oh!

(*She signals to* WILL, *pointing at the ground below her; she mouths her news, sotto voce.*)

Anne. Anne.

WILL: What?

JENNY: Get me out of here!

HODGES [THE ALE]: What will I do with this?

KEMP: Give it to this young—eccentric—

(*He gazes at* WILL.)

What's wrong there?

WILL: I'm opening—closing—

KEMP: Is that lock broken?

WILL: Yes.

HODGES [COMING]: It is?

WILL: No.

HODGES: If ye don't want this—

WILL [FERVENT]: I need it.

(*He takes the ale, and when* HODGES *turns away
he spies out;* JENNY *hisses.*)

JENNY: I'm climbing down!

HODGES: Coming! Coming! I'll break that young bitch's
POPE: I'll have one. Ned?
VOICES [SHOUTING]: Hodges! Hodges!
NED: Yes. Can you quiet them, below?
HODGES [TURNING]: Soon as I—
POPE: Two. Jack? Wait, we—
VOICES: Hodges! Beer and sausage! Hodges!
HODGES [TURNING BACK]: I only have two hands—
HEMING: Make it three.
VOICES: Hodges, Hodges, Hodges, Hodges, Hodges—

(*Which she proceeds to do, slowly disappearing.*)
neck—

(*He hurries out.*)

VOICES [SINGING]:
        —*hey nonny no,*
        When the winds blow and the seas flow?
        Hey nonny no!
NED: Am I to work against that?
KEMP: Do our best.
VOICES:
            Men are fools that wish to die!
            Is it not fine—

NED: Listen to them. Today they guffawed at the death scene.

WILL: Oafs, yes, I agree with—

HEMING: Ned thinks we'd have a glorious stage if we'd only get rid of the damned audience.

POPE: Wasn't the scene, Willie was ogling a wench in the front.

NED: Ogling a—

KEMP: I wasn't ogling a wench.

NED: What were you doing?

KEMP: Humoring the scene.

NED [SHOCKED]: Humoring a death scene? Willie—

KEMP: Well, don't draw it out so.

NED: —I promise you, the next death speech of mine you choose to humor—

HEMING: He'll stab you instead of himself.

NED: I'm not speaking out of vanity!

WILL: Why not?

NED: Did I or any of us invite your comment? Or presence—

WILL: I wept at that scene.

NED [INTERESTED]: Did you really?

(KEMP *looks up.*)

WILL: Yes, I was much taken by you today. And if you have that—gift, to hold another's mind like a kitten by its scruff, tickle and it purrs, squeeze and it cries, be vain. How old are you?

NED: Two and twenty.

WILL: I envy you.

NED: Honored.

WILL: You think if I asked Kemp for a player's share myself he'd say no?

KEMP: He'd say no. Poor bastard has troubles enough.

WILL: Dictatorial bastard, says I can't even watch you work.

NED: Can you act?

WILL: Act, administer the realm, discover new seas—

HEMING: You discover many in this mudhole, boy?

WILL: Oh, even in this mudhole we have one or two, not yet discovered. I mean within, what man is—

(*He lays a finger on* NED's *heart.*)

—lifts its tides in us night and day, but not the— wisdom to know what it is till some fool as bold as this one sails in over dragons to hoist our flag, isn't that what playing is?

NED [STARING]: That is true.

HEMING: Unusual mudhole.

NED: Why can't he watch?

KEMP [CHORTLING]: He can, he can! Watch, act, rule the realm, he'll talk his way into anything. Midnight?

WILL: Midnight.

NED: It's exactly that, and the issue is are we to compromise it to entertain the vulgar, or—

POPE: For God's sake, what's wrong with entertaining the folk? It's what we're for.

NED: It's not what I am for.

KEMP: It's what he's against. Ned, there's your throne.

NED: No, we're either practitioners of an art going back
to the ancients or a pack of clowning beggars, and
I won't be bound to the level of a herd of—

(*His gesture at the singers points him on* ANNE *as
she walks in; she stands, scanning all.*)

—dolts.

WILL: Anne.

(*His eye sidles to the window.* ANNE *is at her come-
liest, and snake-eye bright.*)

ANNE: Now ye wouldn't mean me.

NED [INTERESTED]: No, I—Not in the least. Can I be
of any—

WILL: It's my wife.

NED: Oh.

ANNE: They told me up here, I didn't expect—

KEMP: Come in.

ANNE: —so many men, am I safe, do ye think?

WILL: If anyone is. This is—Will Kemp, and his
assorted rapists—

ANNE: Oh, I'll stay.

(*They bow to her eye, smiling men.*)

WILL: If you wanted to talk with me—

ANNE [PLEASANT]: Yes, how are ye?

WILL: —I can't come to Master Roche now, but I'll—
walk you—

ANNE: Oh, I'll send him home, lad, it wasn't him I
came about.

WILL: Oh?

ANNE: I'm to see all of ye act the play tomorrow, I hear
ye make a better sight than real kings.

NED: We're a nobler breed.

ANNE: I see ye are.

KEMP: Yes, we're crowning one now, with some im-
provements. If you'll forgive us for working—

POPE: Let her watch too.

WILL: No—

HEMING: Have a stool.

WILL: No, she hasn't time, we have—too many children
at home, all—

ANNE: —asleep, pet, and it's not too many.

(*She sits.*)

I don't mind if I do.

KEMP: Ned?

WILL: Anne, it's an intrusion—

NED [PONDERING]: Can you be quiet?

ANNE: As a mouse.

NED: A rare woman. Let her stay, her husband—weeps
at death scenes.

WILL: Thank you again.

(*He makes for the window, and checks the empty roof.*)

NED: Tom, try it without your cross on untimely end—

(*The players confer, in a mutter.*)

KEMP: Comfortable?
ANNE: Oh, yes. Ye're so thoughtful, I'd like—
KEMP: Hm?
ANNE: I'd like an ale, where's Jenny?
KEMP: There's ale coming, but you must be very quiet.
ANNE: I'll be a mouse.
KEMP [SITS]: All right, thus to deprive.

(*A momentary pause.* WILL *sits near* KEMP *and the text; the players begin.*)

HEMING:
   Thus to deprive me of my crown and life,
   To work my downfall and untimely end!
   An uncouth pain torments my grieved soul
   And death arrests the organ of my voice,
   Who, entering at the breach thy sword hath
      made—

(WILL *rises, stares at the text, takes it from* KEMP's *hand.*)

Sacks every vein and artier of my heart.
Insatiate Tamburlaine!

NED [BUT GOOD]:

> The thirst of reign and sweetness of a crown
> Mov'd me to manage arms against thy state.
> Nature, that fram'd us of four elements
> Warring within our breasts for regiment,
> Doth teach us all to have aspiring minds:
> Our souls, whose faculties can comprehend
> The wondrous architecture of the world,
> And measure every wandering planet's course,
> Still climbing after knowledge infinite
> And always moving—

> (He jumps higher, excited.)

> Willie, can I be up here?

KEMP: Yes.

WILL [TRANSFIXED]: Kemp, what is this?

KEMP: Looks fine.

WILL: What is it?

KEMP: New play for London, we're doing scenes tomorrow—

WILL: It's a language for giants. Who wrote it?

KEMP: Friend of Ned's—

NED:

> Nature, that fram'd us of four elements
> Warring within our breasts for regiment,
> Doth teach us all to have aspiring minds—

> (HODGES, in with a trayful of tankards, tiptoes
> around; WILL never takes his eyes from NED.)

Our souls, whose faculties can comprehend
The wondrous architecture of the world,
And measure every wandering planet's course,
Still climbing after knowledge infinite—

HODGES [WHISPERS]: I got them quiet.

NED [FROWNS]:

  —and moving as the restless spheres,
  Will us to—

Missing a beat.

WILL [WITH THE TEXT]: You dropped always, always moving as the restless—

NED: Let me see it.

(*They meet to confer over the text;* HODGES *completes his circuit.*)

ANNE: Where's ye lovely daughter?

HODGES: I don't know where the filthy baggage is. Disappeared. Little trollop, I'll keep her locked in the cellar, off with some—

WILL: She's downstairs, please be quiet.

HODGES: Downstairs where?

WILL: In the—outhouse—

HODGES: Ohhh—

JENNY [OFF]: Help!

(*A silence.*)

WILL: She's stuck.

KEMP: In the outhouse?

WILL: On the roof, damn her. Quick, lend a hand.

KEMP: You—I—don't—

(*He runs after* WILL *to the window, smacks his brow.*)

I see it, yes—oh, you heartless—

HODGES: What, where, stuck where, what's he mean she's—

KEMP [CHORTLING]: Out here, come.

(*He climbs out after* WILL; *they scramble to the edge, to haul* JENNY *up.* ANNE *on the stool twists to wait, coiled.*)

POPE [MEANWHILE]: To wear ourselves?

NED [OUTRAGED]: Now?

POPE: I've got three lines, I've been kneeling for three hours—

NED [SAVAGE]:

> *—always kneeling as the restless dolts*
> *Will us to hang ourselves—*

(*They help* JENNY *back to the window, where* HODGES *has his head out, spluttering questions.*)

> *—and never kneel*
> *Until we reach the ripest fruit of all,*
> *The sweet fruition of an earthly crown!*

(JENNY *stumbles in with the tray,* KEMP *clambering after;* WILL *sits in the window, text in hand, a fatalist.*)

HODGES: —no, but how, how—How did ye get there?
JENNY [A GASP]: I—climbed up—
HODGES [INCREDULOUS]: With a tray?

(JENNY *totters onto a stool, turns, is face to face with* ANNE.)

JENNY: Oh! Good—evening, Anne—
ANNE [PLEASANT]: Good evening, Jenny, are ye laying with my husband?

(*Riveted, all the men stare;* ANNE *waits on* JENNY.)

HODGES [THEN]: What—kind of a—question—
ANNE: He said ask ye, so I came to ask ye. Yes or no, are ye laying with my—

(JENNY *bursts into tears, hysterical.* WILL *jumps in;* ANNE *ignores him.*)

All right, ye are.
NED [ICY]: Kemp, would you tell your friends to go?
KEMP [HELPLESS]: Go.
WILL: I said intrusion, you said rare woman. Anne, you're disrupting a most extraordinary—

(HODGES *catches at him.*)

HODGES: Get her out of my tavern, neither of ye come
    back, I can do without the trouble and the trade—
VOICES [SHOUTING]: Hodges, Hodges, beer and Hodges,
    Hodges—
HODGES: Oh, God in heaven—
KEMP [WEAKER]: Go—
HODGES: Ye piece, get downstairs to work!
ANNE Let her sit, ye peeface, ye brought her up to be a
    piece. Now pay me mind, girl, though I know most
    of ye mind is in ye—dumplings—
KEMP [SITS]: Go.
ANNE: I won't blame ye too bad, anyone can see he's a—

(*She casts her eye briefly at* WILL; *he is intent on
her.*)

—prize, and why wouldn't ye, I did, and as for him
he's a man and they don't grow up, they just think
so if they stick it into any tub of lard with legs.
Snap ye fingers they come, I had them making
eyes at me here, but ye think he gives two thoughts
to ye? He'd sooner sit and hear speeches no one
can make head or tail of. All the same, this one is
mine. I want him, I'm not giving him to ye, lass,
I know ye're a ninny but try to remember, because
—now mind me—if ye once come near enough for
him to smell ye again, and ye don't smell all that

good, I'll pluck both ye squinty eyes out and scrub
ye skin on the stones in the river.

WILL: Not quite a mouse.

KEMP: Done?

ANNE: Yes, it's all I came to say. Thank ye all, I'm
sorry I took ye time—

WILL: Anne, this is no way to a man's heart or—other
organs—

ANNE: Not quite a man.

(WILL *stands rigid.*)

JENNY: Squinty!

ANNE: No one's told ye?

(*She passes* JENNY *to leave,* JENNY *hits her over
the head with the tray, and the fight is on; they
grapple, fall, roll on the floor in a hubbub of many
voices, clawing at each other's face and clothes, the
men making way.* ANNE *straddles her, pulling hair,
and* HODGES *intervenes (*"Let go, I'll hit her, let
go!"*);* ANNE *hits him backhand;* HODGES *gives her
a kick,* WILL *clutching the text gives* HODGES *a kick,
they swing fists, grapple, fall over* ANNE; JENNY
crawls out but ANNE *seizes her skirt, which rips
loose, and falls upon her to pummel;* ARTHUR *climbs
on a stool for refuge;* KEMP *cheers them on (*"Upper garment, get the upper garment!"*) as* HEMING
holds ANNE's *fists, she struggles, and* WILL *tackling*
HEMING *brings him down;* HODGES *half covers and*

half beats JENNY *as she crawls;* NED *pulls free of*
POPE's *clutch in a rage* ("*Look for me below, or
even London!*") *and stalks out over bodies;* JENNY
breaking away collides into ARTHUR's *stool,* ARTHUR
topples, KEMP *catches him.* JENNY *escapes out,
half-naked and shrieking, with* ANNE *in pursuit; the
shrieks rise, off.* KEMP *runs after them, to a sound
of bodies tumbling downstairs; he skips back.*)

KEMP: Not a stitch on her, lovely sight, come, come!
Arthur, come, study real women in moments of
stress—

(*All the* PLAYERS *run out, to a hubbub downstairs;
it dies away.* WILL *is left alone, on the floor. He
sits up, feels his nose, gets to his knees, looks
around, and crawls, picking up a few loose pages
of the text; he puts them in order, scanning each.*)

WILL: The wondrous architecture of the world. Which
I suppose includes females.

(*He crawls for another page, scans it.*)

An uncouth pain. Is more like it.

(*Text finally in sequence, he gets up with it, walks
to the stools with the candles, drops the text upon
it. He searches, picks up his jacket in a corner,*

*comes back to the candles, and pinches one out;
about to pinch the other, he pauses over the text.)*

An uncouth pain.

*(After some thought he pinches the candle out,
leaving only moonlight; he remains motionless. He
then essays a foot on the stool, a hand up.)*

An uncouth pain—

(Presently he has a slow whispering try at it.)

*—torments my grieved soul
And death—*

(The moonlight fades.)

—arrests the organ of my voice—

END OF THE ACT

ACT II

To willful men
The injuries that they themselves procure
Must be their schoolmasters.

SCENE 1

A BANISTER AT THE PLATFORM; BELOW IT, A TABLE WITH
BENCH, A STOOL OR TWO.

ANNE, BUTTONING HER BODICE AFTER NURSING, COMES
DOWNSTAIRS WITH SOILED DIAPER CLOUTS, DUMPS THEM,
STACKS AND TAKES AWAY DIRTY PLATES ON THE TABLE,
AND SITS THINKING; HER EYEBROW IS BANDAGED.

OLD JOHN, A VAGUE PALE MAN, SHUFFLES IN WITH A
CANDLE; A MURMUR OF VOICES CONTINUES BEHIND HIM.

JOHN: Ye brought a bite to the old girl, didn't ye.

(ANNE *nods.*)

And the twins?
ANNE: Two bites.

(*She takes up her darning, to thread a needle.*)

JOHN: If ye eye hurts, ye shouldn't use it.

ANNE: Whose should I use?

JOHN [A PAUSE]: Is it my Will?

ANNE: Hm?

JOHN: That troubles ye.

ANNE: Oh, never.

JOHN [RESTLESS]: Eh, where can he be, the schoolmaster'll soon be off—

ANNE: Makes me feel old, ugly, I mean less to him and less to him, and whatever I do is mistakes, why would it trouble me?

JOHN: Was never easy with the boy, and this teaching, we had to—woo him to anything we wanted—

ANNE: I've been wooing him since his teens, when do I get him?

(*A bell is shaken, upstairs; they listen.*)

JOHN: The old girl wants one of us.

(ROCHE *enters, with a letter;* GILBERT, *a brute in bloody garb, follows, picking his teeth.*)

ROCHE: I fear I shall look very foolish in this with Sir Thomas.

(ANNE *rises, takes a chamberpot, goes up at the banister.*)

JOHN: Eh, where can he be—

GILBERT: I don't know where the Christ he can be, I hope dead.

(*He sits, heels mud off his boots.*)

JOHN: No way to talk of ye brother—

ANNE: Gilbert, ye slob, out back, don't track up my floor.

(*She goes off.*)

ROCHE: If it were not for my letter of recommendation to— Should I read it?

(GILBERT *looks at him.*)

No.

GILBERT [GOING]: Had to take on the whole kill myself, ye think he makes ye look foolish? he makes me feel like a wet fart—

ROCHE: John, if I were perhaps to leave it—

JOHN: I don't know what to say, schoolmaster. Times are bad enough, here I'm with debts over me—

ROCHE: Yes, I—

JOHN: —and my old girl up there, as ye know, I'm not well myself—

(GILBERT *comes back, with a full mug.*)

GILBERT: I'm sick of doing his work, damn him, all of ye counting on me to carry the whole of it—

JOHN: But ye got them all?

GILBERT: I got them all. The hides are in the wagon.

JOHN: It's as I say, schoolmaster. Here he's raising a
family, and debts over me, isn't it only right he—

(ANNE *comes down with a tray of dirty dishes.*)

ANNE: Master Roche don't want to hear more of our
troubles, he heard them all. Stay a bit yet, I'll give
ye some cakes and—
ROCHE: No, no, but—Tell Will I am seeing Sir Thomas
in the morning, with my letter—

(ANNE *takes the letter, sits, handles it.*)

ANNE: What's it say?
ROCHE: It says what I truly think, but is he not inter-
ested?
ANNE: Says, rub me and make a wish. It's so—simple—

(*She slaps it down, takes up the tray.*)

ROCHE [LOW]: Anne, I am worried for his sake. I think
perhaps this house is—oppressive, so much—
ANNE: I can't be someone I'm not.
ROCHE: —sickness and decline, I meant. Urge him to—
take you away to a new—
ANNE: It's a grand idea, I'll tell him.

(SUSANNA *in nightgown darts in above, downstairs,
weaves among them, and runs out.*)

SUSANNA: Papa, Papa—

ANNE: Ears like a little bat.

ROCHE: Eh?

ANNE: Ye can tell him yeself. She—listens, watches,
  I don't know what—

WILL [OFF]: No, no, no, I'll—

SUSANNA [OFF]: —yes, yes, ye have to—

WILL [OFF]: —recite instead.

(*He totters in with* SUSANNA *sprawling over his
shoulder, the text under his arm, a few flowers in
his hand.*)

For I, the chiefest lamp in all the earth—

(GILBERT *is up at once;* WILL *and* ANNE *with the
tray confront each other in silence, then* ANNE *goes
out past him.*)

GILBERT: Ye figging sneak, where were ye?

WILL:

> *First rising in the east with mild aspect*
> *But fixed now in the meridian line—*

GILBERT: What?

WILL [SWINGS SUSANNA]:

> *Will send up fire to your turning spheres!*

GILBERT: Left the whole kill to me, who'd ye run off
  to see?

WILL: Language, language, brother, does it exalt you?
  Master Roche.

GILBERT: I want to know where ye went!

JOHN: Yes, where?

WILL: To the play. I said I—

GILBERT: Play!

SUSANNA: Why can't I go—

GILBERT: Ye sneaky fart, ye said ye had someone to—

WILL: I had to see Kemp.

JOHN: Went to a play—

GILBERT: While I was skinning the lot?

ANNE [IN]: Ye'll wake the twins, ye big noise, sit down out of the way.

(*She pushes him back, half takes* SUSANNA, *who clings.*)

Susie, back to bed.

SUSANNA: I'm hungry, why can't I see the play—

WILL: Didn't she eat?

SUSANNA: No.

ANNE: Of course she ate. Susanna, ye heard what—

(GILBERT *flings the mug at a corner, it shatters. After a silence* ANNE *goes, kneels; she picks up the pieces.*)

Gilbert, will ye do me a favor? Get married, either move out or bring me a helper.

GILBERT: Move out, ye'll all starve.

JOHN: I'll help ye.

(*The bell is shaken, upstairs.*)

GILBERT: Comes in here, loving her up so, why don't
he do his share for her keep?

ANNE: Susanna, ye heard what I said.

GILBERT: Had the sense she was born with she'd spit
in ye eye.

WILL [UNLOADS HER]: Yes. Say hello and goodbye to our
guest, I'll come up.

(SUSANNA *stares at* ROCHE.)

WILL: No?

(SUSANNA *sucks her thumb*.)

Talks less than Gilbert but the quality is better—

(GILBERT *stands up*; WILL *puts himself behind*
ROCHE.)

GILBERT: Get my hands on ye I won't be talking at all!

WILL: Protect your protégé—

ROCHE: Will, I did wish—unless your interest in it has
diminished—to come to an understanding on Redditch. My letter—

(*The bell is shaken again*; ANNE, *turning with the
pieces in her apron, stops; all listen.*)

JOHN: I'll go.

(*He climbs at the banister;* ANNE *starts off opposite.*)

ANNE: Upstairs, chick.
SUSANNA: Ye said we'd see the play—
ANNE: I said tomorrow, now get to—
WILL: Marigolds. I picked them for you.

(ANNE *looks at them in his hand, impassive.*)

ANNE: Don't give me—things—

(*She bears the pieces out;* WILL *stands with the
flowers.*)

WILL [THEN]: What letter, sir?
ROCHE: For Sir Thomas, he will sign his name.

(WILL *exchanges with him, flowers for letter.*)

I thought you should see it beforehand. I know
that once he has spoken with you, the outcome is
hardly in doubt. Unless of course you—
WILL: It's a handsome letter. Gilbert, I would like you
to pay close attention, it begins with—
GILBERT: Stick it up ye ass.
WILL: I don't—see that phrase, no, it begins less ar-
dently—

ROCHE: Then are we to bring it to Sir Thomas in the morning?

WILL: In the morning seems—hasty—

(ANNE *comes in with a rag.*)

ANNE [IMPATIENT]: Get to bed, get to bed.

SUSANNA: Papa said he'd tell me a story.

ROCHE: It is most convenient for him in the morning—

WILL: Not for me, I—must help Gilbert in the morning.

GILBERT [GRIM]: And hereafter.

WILL: I don't think we'll be together there.

GILBERT: Where?

WILL: The hereafter.

(*He exchanges again with* ROCHE, *letter for flowers.*)

ROCHE: But what shall I tell Sir Thomas?

WILL: Tell him I won't know until I talk with Anne.

(ANNE, *wiping the floor, looks up.*)

ROCHE: I understand, yes, yes, I did not mean to press. Now I must be going. Goodbye—

SUSANNA: Hello.

ROCHE: Ha. Makes sport of me already and has yet to

come to school. Good night.

(ROCHE *bows himself out.*)

SUSANNA: He's a funny old man—
WILL: Yes. Marigolds, have one, I picked them for—
    Not you, was it Gilbert, no—
GILBERT: Watch out.
WILL: —now who could I—
SUSANNA: Mommy, ye silly.
WILL: Ah, yes. Give them to Mommy.

(SUSANNA *takes them.*)

Marigolds, I picked them for you, Mommy.

(ANNE *looks at him, impassive.*)

Cat has Mommy's tongue, nothing to say?
ANNE: Yes. Ye got the gall of a pig.

(*She accepts the flowers;* SUSANNA *runs back to* WILL.)

WILL [CONFIDES]: She's liking me better—
ANNE: Get me a mug, if ye can hold onto it.

(*She tosses the wet rag to* GILBERT, *who takes it out, and she brings the flowers to the table;* WILL *swings* SUSANNA.)

Did ye eat there?

WILL: No, I drank there. Up to bed—

SUSANNA: Tell me the story first, tell me the—

WILL: Short and sweet, there was a beautiful young
girl, short and sweet, whose name was—ah—

SUSANNA: Susanna.

WILL: Yes, and she was called—

ANNE: I'll get ye supper.

WILL: —La Belle Dame of Shottery for short. Now her
stepmother—

(ANNE *going out turns.*)

—married her off to a certain young man, who—

SUSANNA: What was his name?

WILL: —whose name—was Peregrine Pig, he looked
like a pig, with a big pig nose and wee pig eyes
and a—wig like a pig—

SUSANNA: A wig like a—

WILL: —and he swilled and he swigged because he was
so pig-headed, but—

SUSANNA: Did he have a tail?

WILL: Yes, it's a—

(GILBERT *comes in with an empty mug, but* ANNE
is listening.)

—wriggly tale—

GILBERT: Here.

SUSANNA: What was his hands?

WILL: Pig feet. And—

SUSANNA: What was his feet?

WILL: Pig, very pig feet, and he put one in his mouth
every time he opened—

SUSANNA: What was his mouth?

WILL: Pig lips, blub, blub, he thpoke thith way, with
hith foot in hith mouth, and—

(ANNE *sits.*)

GILBERT: Why are ye listening to his garbage?

WILL: —and—after he ate the garbage he'd come to
woo her, all he could thay wath, I oink you, I oink
you—

SUSANNA [DELIGHTED]: I oink you?

WILL: I oink you, yes, and his bride, seeing how repulthive he wath, would—

SUSANNA: What's pulthive?

WILL: Repulthive. Like Gilbert. She was so—

(JOHN *comes down as* GILBERT *hurls the mug at*
WILL, *who ducks; it shatters.*)

GILBERT: I told ye watch out!

JOHN: Gilbert, are ye crazy?

GILBERT: I've had enough of ye lip, gabbing, handing
out flowers, telling stories, stories—

ANNE: Get the broom, ye fool.

GILBERT: Get it yeself! I'm going down the tavern.

(He strides out, and the bell is shaken, upstairs.
WILL *turns to look up;* JOHN *crosses with a sigh,*
to climb at the banister.)

SUSANNA: Then what?

ANNE: Yes, then what?

WILL: She would—hide in her broom closet. Till one
day she peeked and saw him crying, I'm tho dith-
guthting, if the'd only kith me oneth: and what
did she say?

SUSANNA: What?

WILL: She said, I'll kiss the silly pig, and she did, and
his tail fell off.

SUSANNA: Ah.

WILL: And he lotht—his lisp, his snout melted away,
the pigment in his skin grew bright, his eyes grew
like two suns, and he stood up: do you know what
he was?

SUSANNA: A prince!

WILL: A prince, under a witch's spell, till she kissed
him as a pig. Which is another magic, called loving, very—complicated. And they lived happily—

SUSANNA [WITH HIM]: —ever after?

WILL: —ever after, until they were old lovers, and died
of complications. Now upstairs, upstairs, and asleep
in two shakes of a pig's tail, go—

*(*SUSANNA *scrambles upstairs escaping his slaps on*
her butt; she turns back, above.)

SUSANNA [DELIGHTED]: I oink you?
WILL: I oink you too. Go.

(SUSANNA *goes;* ANNE *and* WILL *are alone.*)

ANNE [THEN]: A prince, yes, ye bastard.
WILL [THEN]: I oink you.
ANNE: She kissed him, ye said, did he kiss her?

(JOHN *reappears with the chamberpot, lidded;* ANNE *rises to take it.*)

JOHN: She says what keeps breaking?
WILL: Vows. How is she tonight?
ANNE [GOING]: She'll outlive the twins—
JOHN: I wouldn't be sure, when ye're her age ye're—

(ANNE *is gone.*)

—all old bones.
WILL [WITH THE TEXT]: Yes. Sacks every vein and artier.
JOHN: I'm glad if ye're taking the teaching.
WILL: Eh?
JOHN: I know the tanning isn't—for ye, no, good
    enough for Gilbert or me all my life, but times
    change, the good times are all gone—
WILL: Were there any?
JOHN: Oh yes, yes, why, ye have ye good times, don't
    ye?
WILL [THINKS]: No. I'm like a cross-eyed idiot keeps

marching into posts. Pa, why can I never—ask
you—

JOHN: What?

WILL: —so many things, I don't know which, the—
point of it all, is that answerable now, what was—

JOHN: Oh, ye mother's the deep one. Or was, I'm—

WILL: What was the best of it?

JOHN: The best. Best, well, I—lose things, but I remember—yes, bailiff, in the scarlet and fur, all the
aldermen in their gowns leading us through the
streets, and ye toddled along, three or was it—
Four, ye were born the spring of the plague, the
plague, yes, ye mother so anxious over ye because
we'd lost the two girls before and it was a—dread
summer, crosses in red chalk on all the doors—

WILL: The best of it was the plague?

(ANNE *bears a trayful in.*)

JOHN: No, bailiff, I—wore the scarlet trimmed with—

ANNE: Fur.

JOHN: Fur. Well. No sense to that, no.

(*He pauses at the banister.*)

I was saying what, I—lose things now, I—Ah. Ye
won't regret the teaching. Good night—

WILL: Good night.

(JOHN *goes;* WILL *stands, with the text;* ANNE *sets
his supper down, puts the marigolds in a mug.*)

ANNE: Ye're taking it?

WILL: My father, Tamburlaine, in the scarlet and fur.
My God, what becomes of us?

(*He throws the text on the table, sits, and fingers
it.* ANNE *sits with her darning.* WILL *begins to read.*)

ANNE [THEN]: Ye said talk.

WILL [READING]: Yes.

ANNE: Are ye taking it?

WILL [READING]: It?

ANNE: The teaching.

(*She waits.*)

Will ye put that away and—

(*She sweeps the pages away.*)

—mind me, if ye're sober?

(WILL *gathers them up again.*)

WILL: Of course. I'm drunk only on this play, which
you disrupted there too, it tells me to pillage cities
to come at my desire: and what I'm asked is
walk behind our schoolmaster's—sheaf of dutiful
bones—

ANNE: Are ye taking it?

WILL: —into Sir Thomas's palm. It's not enough, no, it's—

ANNE: Then why talk, ye liar.

WILL: Don't—

(ANNE *bites the thread off, rises, slaps the darning down.*)

—call me liar, and—

ANNE: Damn liar.

WILL: —sit down!

ANNE [DANGEROUS]: Mind it, lad, I'm not ye little wench—

WILL: I didn't say lie down.

(ANNE *stands inarticulate, then wheels to leave.*)

Here, throw this, one more won't matter.

(*He tosses a mug, she catches it; for a moment she is tempted.*)

ANNE: I don't throw things, sweet.

WILL: Not when a ladylike fit of fingernails will do. I admired the two of you, such gentle blood I saw. Will you join me?

(*He puts the text aside;* ANNE *is moveless.*)

I said it's not enough, not that I wouldn't, sit or
not.

(ANNE *brings the mug back, sits opposite him.*)

Nor that I would, either.

ANNE: Oh, God help me.

WILL: Now we can patch up our differences again—

ANNE: If I made a fool of myself there it's my doing,
but ye, ye damn peacock—

WILL: —over a pleasant conversation—

ANNE: —ye make such a fool of me every time—

WILL: —that leads nowhere, or—

ANNE: —ye say a word!

(*She strikes the needle into his wrist; he writhes
away.*)

WILL: God—damn—

ANNE: Don't lose the needle, please.

WILL: Certainly not, I'm deeply imbedded to you.

ANNE [IRONIC]: I'm sorry if I give ye pain.

WILL: Oh, pain is always a pleasure, it reminds me
we're not the—compliant vapors that drift in and
out of my daydreams, now how much of it can
you bear?

ANNE: Give me it.

(*She catches at the needle, rises.*)

WILL: I mean I've been pondering a different compact
with you, a conversation we can get our teeth into.

ANNE [TURNS]: What?

WILL: Truth, all or nothing, no lies, no question evaded,
no mercies or delicacies, go down in the slop as—
honest as pigs, and look at what each of us is married to.

(*He waits.*)

No?

ANNE: Why?

WILL: To see if it's enough.

(*He waits.*)

No?

ANNE [A PAUSE]: Yes.

WILL: Then sit.

(ANNE *lifts the darning off the stool, sits.*)

ANNE: I'm sitting. Start.

WILL: You.

ANNE: How many times did ye lay with her?

WILL: Fifteen. Twenty.

ANNE: Why?

WILL: Is that a question? I was agog for her—dump-
lings, my hands itched.

ANNE: Is she the only one?

WILL: Well, that's no answer. No, she's not the only
    one, I was—

ANNE: Who else?

WILL: Tumble and tell?

ANNE: Ye said everything.

WILL: Yes. You don't know them though, one at Snit-
    terfield, one—

ANNE: How many?

WILL [RECALLING]: —five, six—

ANNE: I'll kill ye!

(*She comes at him, he slips around the table.*)

WILL: No more questions?

ANNE [GRITTILY]: Oh, I have questions, pet, yes—

WILL: Then don't kill the goose that laid—Et cetera.

ANNE: Six is it, ha?

WILL: Seven.

ANNE [HITS THE TABLE]: Why, ye think ye're a great
    bull down there, ye're not—

WILL: Is that a complaint?

ANNE: No—yes, if that's all I thought about, now an-
    swer me—

WILL [A KNIFE]: Compared to what?

ANNA [STOPPED]: Ye know what, I told ye, the—one
    before we—

WILL: Compared to—ancient history, it grows longer
    with time. Who since?

ANNE: Since we—?

WILL: Since we.

(ANNE *sits, half averted, very reluctant.*)

ANNE: One.
WILL: Who?
ANNE: Once.
WILL: Who?
ANNE: Sandy.
WILL: Sandells!

(*He spins in disbelief, stops.*)

Compared to Sandells?
ANNE: Oh, yes.

(WILL *is dumb; her eye now taunts him.*)

Ye daren't ask?
WILL: How—bully is—old friend Sandells?

(ANNE *shows with her palms apart.*)

Needn't kill me, I'll kill myself—
ANNE: Starts there.

(*She inches her palms apart, wider, wider, until
she laughs.*)

Oh God, ye're a baby—
WILL: It's all foreskin, was there a once?

(ANNE *no longer laughs; she then nods.*)

When?

ANNE: This summer.

WILL: How?

ANNE: He—he—put my hand on it, I—was—

WILL: Captured.

ANNE: Yes.

WILL: Womanly compassion.

ANNE: No.

WILL: Higgledy piggledy, two in the stew, now don't
be so cleanly with me, please?

ANNE: It's not the same. Did I have a husband so—
glad to do it, or able?

WILL [TERSE]: I'm able, ask.

ANNE: Which one? Anyone but me, so many ye—No,
why, why did—

WILL: Curiosity?

ANNE: I wasn't enough?

WILL: No, half the world is female—parts, I didn't
think I should go to my grave in ignorance.

ANNE: Ignorance.

WILL: Of all others. Well, that's also no answer—

ANNE [SCORNFUL]: Ye find such a goggle of difference?

WILL: Some.

ANNE: What's so darling damn different?

(WILL *looks at her, glinty.*)

Tell me, tell me—
WILL: Size, degree of—lubricity, color—taste—

(ANNE *closes her eyes.*)

—grip, friskiness—So on.
ANNE: And theirs is—better?
WILL: Different.
ANNE: Better?
WILL: Some.

(ANNE *puts a hand over her face, sits, without a move or sound, till* WILL *repents.*)

Anne, Anne—
ANNE: Never mind!
WILL [BITEY]: Yes, don't cry.
ANNE: Is that ye plan, now?
WILL: What?
ANNE: Half the world?
WILL: It's why we're talking.

(A *pause.*)

Was it very—exciting?
ANNE: Sandy?

(WILL *nods.*)

Shall I tell ye the truth?

WILL: No.

ANNE: I didn't come, lad.

WILL [A PAUSE]: Thank you.

ANNE: I kept seeing ye ugly face, I turned like a clam, then.

(WILL *now comes, sits opposite her; he pokes at the text.*)

WILL [THEN]: I said died of complications, didn't I.

ANNE: Ye didn't tell her it was seven, twenty times each—

WILL: Not with all.

ANNE: Why not, they didn't think much of ye?

WILL: Gets boring.

ANNE: For a boy I been feeling sorry for, ye—have a grand gift to surprise me—

WILL: But God gives each of us a fruit, and one way or another I mean to eat it, before I die, before I die.

ANNE: When did ye start on them, I didn't guess one?

WILL: While you were—I'm sorry—carrying the—

(*He indicates upstairs.*)

ANNE: Twins.

(*She nods.*)

Yes, that I knew, I had them all by myself, yes.

And if ye hands itched for me ye'd—get the milk
keeps them alive, not too pleasing to a lover, lad,
is it.

WILL: It's not that.

ANNE: And I'm running around here with diapers and
dishrags, nobody's picture of a—doxy ye can't keep
ye hands off—

WILL: Not that.

ANNE: Ye couldn't wait, what?

WILL: Oh, I could wait, yes, but—Not take a wife any
longer who suckles and swaddles and wipes me
like a babe in public, no.

(A *wait*.)

ANNE: Ye liked it, lad.

WILL: Don't call me that. I'm not always seventeen.
I'm not—yours, you said I was, I'm mine, and
out of whatever love you stalked in as mother
tigress tonight, your tongue licks me with con-
tempt. I like it: I loathe it. Be strong, be strong
with—others, you're throttling a lover to death.
And that I think is the answer.

(A *silence, their eyes on each other across the
table*.)

ANNE: Is that—the worst ye have to say?

(WILL *gazes at her.*)

It's a question, la—love.
WILL: No.
ANNE: What else?

(WILL *picks up the text, stands up.*)

WILL: No, the game is over.
ANNE: No it isn't, not till both of us say, and I have
      to know.

(WILL *is silent.*)

Tell me, ye—milksop, what's the worst ye think,
ye'll leave me?
WILL: I think, she's older, she'll die first.

(ANNE *hides her face in a hand, and this time does
cry; it begins with a jerky breath, she keeps the
crying in her gut, but at last it breaks her open.*
WILL *comes back, tosses the text on the table,
stands behind her racked figure, to finger her nape.*)

ANNE: Don't—touch—
WILL: Anne, nothing's impossible—the schoolteaching,
      family and fidelity, even Gilbert is possible—if I
      can—

(*With both hands he caresses her hair, ears, eyes.*)

—ripen with it, that's all I mean by enough. Your
cheek is wet. Is that the only thing?

(*He draws her body back against his groin; she
stiffens, slowly moves against him.*)

ANNE: None of—ye business—
WILL: Oh, I think it is.

(*His hands come down over her, bosom, belly,
then he twists to the candle; he sees the marigolds,
picks a few, sits beside her, and puts a flower in
her hair.*)

That's for the dishrags.

(*She bites at his hand; he puts another into her
bodice.*)

For the diapers, Yes, he—

(*A last flower in his fingers, he twists to blow out
the candle.*)

—did kiss her. You have no idea where I mean
to put this one—

(*ANNE begins to laugh, in the dark; it is a marvel-
lous laugh, also up out of her gut, hearty and pro-
longed; but it ends presently in a little gasp.*)

ANNE: Not here—
WILL: Here.

(*Silence.*)

SCENE 2

A MUTTER OF TWO OR THREE VOICES, AS MOONLIGHT
STEALS IN ON THE TREE. FULK, MEG, AND KEMP CIRCLE
IN WITH CROSSBOWS; THEY HALT, TO PEER BEHIND.

KEMP [WHISPERS]: Will?
FULK: Where'd the boy go to?
MEG: Will?

> (*They scatter off, searching.* WILL *breaks in, reeling, falls, hits at the earth, stumbles up and across, drops to his knees.*)

WILL: Oh, my—Christ, what have I—done, where can
I flee, with the humpback and twisted foot of love?

> (*He is racked, on his knees. In the shadows* KEMP *circles back in.*)

KEMP [CALLS]: Hey, you fellow felon, Will?

> (*He spies him, comes.*)

If we get a deer I'll—

(*He stops, squats to stare.*)

Are you sick, or—

WILL: Sick, I've just committed suicide—

KEMP: What?

WILL: Oh God, nothing looks the same before and after
the act of love. I made her a promise, to be a
schoolmaster, and my gut won't keep it down, I'm
like—water and jiggling bones. I ran out of the
house in such a panic I—Kemp, what in God's
name is evil in me?

KEMP: You're not evil.

WILL: Am I such a lunatic then?

KEMP: Only here. London is full of us, nobody notices.

WILL: London.

(*It brings his head up;* FULK *circles in, with* MEG.)

FULK: No talking from here down.

KEMP: Which way?

FULK [LEADING]: To the river, they come down there to
drink.

MEG [FOLLOWING]: Sometimes.

FULK: Every night.

MEG: Sometimes.

FULK: I say every night, another word and I'll wrap a
stick around ye—

KEMP: We'll talk after, come, lad—

(*They go off.* WILL *remains, alone.*)

WILL: London. Be still, you pulsing toad in me, be still.
Is there one face that swims in my tear I cannot
now see dead and out of my way? such murder is
in me: and in all the swarms that copulate, lift
any stone the bugs are busy as little soldiers and
butchers. Carnage is half the soul of the quietest
leaf. Which falls, breathing its counsel, Destroy:
all is reborn, April rises from its bed sweet with
the rotted flesh of log and corpse, the worm is reborn in birdsong, and all creation works its mira-
cles in the hand of destruction: then why am I to
be out of its law, and merciful? when I come here,
here, to breathe with all that—

(*He breaks off, peering.*)

Who's that?
JENNY: It's me.

(*She comes into the moonlight, her eye and thumb
bandaged.*)

WILL: Where did you come from?
JENNY: I followed ye.
WILL: Why?
JENNY: I'm lonely. What were ye hollering for, ye want
to be caught?
WILL: Yes.
JENNY: What?
WILL: I must undo—undo a promise I made to teach,

to be a schoolmaster—

(*He takes her hand.*)

Jenny, I'm—

JENNY: Ow. She bit me there—

WILL: I'm sorry.

JENNY: —a bite like that can be very bad, some bites are poisonous. And the old bastard took a board to me, he beat me too—

(*She clutches him, listening.*)

What's that?

WILL: Fulk.

(*A pause; she caresses him.*)

JENNY: Ye—feel like?

WILL: Aren't you afraid of her bite?

JENNY: How would she know?

WILL: I would tell her.

JENNY: Oh. I don't—know why I came, then.

(*She drifts from him, waits.*)

I don't know why I'm going. No one there even to talk to—

WILL: Talk to me.

JENNY: Why?

WILL: I'm lonely.

(*He twists away.*)

I don't, don't, don't know what to do—
JENNY: Ye don't want me.
WILL: Not true.
JENNY: Ye do want me.
WILL: Jenny, man and wife put out roots that invade
    each other, children too, till there's—such a root-
    bind on us all—
JENNY: Eh?
WILL: —we're one flesh, not separable except—by
    bleeding—
JENNY: Ahh—
WILL: —and I can pull loose and bleed, or I can stran-
    gle—
JENNY [A PAUSE]: Ye mean, leave them?
WILL: Or strangle in the feeble arms of children, what
    shall I do?
JENNY [WATCHES HIS MISERY]: I could tell ye.
WILL: But you'll be wooed by many others, with clearer
    heads, you're an eyeful of pleasure.
JENNY: Oh, these. It's when ye have a child they get
    real big.
WILL: The world has much to look forward to.
JENNY [A PAUSE]: I have a child.
WILL [STARES]: What?
JENNY: She's three now. She lives in Bristol, with a
    nice family, she thinks it's her mommy. They let
    me name her, though, I named her Clarinda. Ye
    like that name?
WILL: Yes—

JENNY: She's pretty too, ye could eat her, curly hair and all, very yellow. Or it was, they said it would change, and this year he—wouldn't let me go, because I—because I didn't want to give her to them to start with, he—he—

WILL: Yes.

JENNY: —and I can't—see her without—

(*She weeps.*)

I want her to know. I want her to know. I want her, that's all—

(*She weeps herself out.* WILL *waits, attentive.*)

WILL: Yes. (*He takes her hand.*)

JENNY: Ow.

(FULK *is heard calling; the moonlight darkens.*)

FULK [OFF]: Will. We got a deer. Will.

JENNY: I don't want to see him, I look terrible—

WILL: Go the other way, I'll hold him off.

FULK [NEARER]: Will. Where in hell are ye now?

(JENNY *runs one way,* WILL *moves the other.*)

WILL: I'm over here—

(*In the shadows* JENNY *falls, to the iron clang of*

the trap; she screams.)

Jenny! What is it?

(*He runs scrambling to her; she screams terribly.*)

Oh Christ.

(*He works to pry it open.*)

Fulk! Fulk!
JENNY [SCREAMING]: I, I, I, I—
WILL: Fulk!

(FULK *runs in.*)

FULK: What's wrong?
WILL: Jenny, they set a trap—
FULK: Oh, Jesus.
WILL: Get the other side.
JENNY [SCREAMING]: I couldn't see—

(RICHARDS *runs in opposite with a knife.*)

RICHARDS: Now then—

(*He falters.*)

It's Hodges' girl—

WILL: Help me!

(*They pull the trap open;* KEMP *and* MEG *run in, and see* RICHARDS.)

MEG: Yiyy—

(*They separate and flee.*)

WILL: Move, move—
JENNY [SCREAMING]: I, I, I can't—

(FULK *pulls her free, the trap clangs again.*)

FULK: Oh God, that foot looks bad.
JENNY [SCREAMING]: I couldn't see—
WILL: Blood, I can't tell what it's—
RICHARDS: I—didn't mean—
FULK: What'll we do with her?
WILL: Is anyone at the house?
RICHARDS: I didn't know it'd be her, or so—
WILL [HARD]: Is there help at the house?
RICHARDS: Sir Thomas.
FULK: Hand ourselves over, boy?
WILL: It was my worst intention, yes, take her to Sir
Thomas.

(*They lift* JENNY, *screaming, and carry her off; the moonlight dies out; the thud of a drum is heard.*)

SCENE 3

THE DRUM GROWS, LIKE A SUMMONS; A BUZZ OF GOSSIP-
ING VOICES RISES TO THE BUSTLE OF A CROWD AT THE
FULL. DAYLIGHT SLOWLY UP.

A THRONG OF TOWNSPEOPLE IS MILLING ABOUT THE
STOCKS; THE HANDS AND FEET STICKING OUT ARE THOSE
OF FULK, WILL, AND RICHARDS, ALL IN AN EXHAUSTION OF
PAIN, WILL IN A SAVAGE PONDERING. HODGES AND SANDELLS
STAND TALKING, AND SUSANNA SITS SUCKING ON A CANDY
STICK. A TOWNSMAN WITH A LUTE IS TAUNTING.

TOWNSMAN:
> *I cannot now recall things,*
> *Live but a fool to pine:*
> *'Twas I that beat the bush—*

FULK [THROUGH PAIN]: I'll beat ye bush, I get out of
here.

(*The* TOWNSMAN *laughs, moves off, plucking.*)

SUSANNA: Papa. Papa.
WILL [THROUGH PAIN]: Go home, ladybug.

SUSANNA: Papa, what are ye sitting there for, all day?

FULK: That's a fine way to rear a child, in ignorance of
the customs of her country.

WILL: I instruct by example, like Sir Thomas.

FULK: Agh, that stick.

WILL: I'm making a ballad. To his clarity of soul.

FULK: Oh? Say it.

WILL: I need a rhyme for stick.

FULK: Hey, Richards, what rhymes with stick, ye prune?

(BERRY *passes by, among* TOWNSPEOPLE.)

RICHARDS [THROUGH PAIN]: Berry, isn't it time yet?

BERRY: Soon now.

WILL: Is there news of Jenny?

BERRY: Ye'll hear.

RICHARDS: I only did my duty. And for what?—shown
off to the town in disgrace next to two thieves—

FULK: Ah, ye're just like our blessed savior.

HODGES: Ye're a filthy pair of rogues, ye'll be meat for
the hangman if ye keep—

SANDELLS: Hush, man, his daughter is here.

SUSANNA: No, I'm not.

HODGES: I've got a daughter, there she is in her bed
tossing in pain, and what am I to do about it?

WILL: Go hit her with a board. It's very soothing.

HODGES: What?

WILL: If not to her, to you.

(HODGES *approaches, spits on* WILL.)

BERRY: Easy—

HODGES: I bring her up to be a good decent girl, and this
piss in his pants turns her into a whore!

WILL: You know better.

HODGES: Eh?

WILL: Truth, truth. Tell the truth and—

HODGES [STARES]: I hope I'm there when they hang ye!

(*He marches out.*)

SANDELLS: Maybe he's right, to be rid of ye'd be the
best thing for Anne.

WILL: Or for you?

SANDELLS: If ye had any thought for her ye wouldn't
be here, ye'd be home or at work like the rest of
us, not off rioting with a wench that's not ye own—

WILL: Oh, God. I lie, he lies, you lie—

(ANNE, *her face like stone, enters with a bulky
sack, and sets it down.*)

ANNE: Susie, I don't want ye here now.

SANDELLS: I was just telling her that, and—

(*He takes* SUSANNA *by the hand.*)

Can I take her home for ye?

ANNE: She knows the way.

WILL: Yes, don't try any lewd handy-pandy with the
child.

SANDELLS: Eh?

WILL: I said give her back her hand, she's too young.

(SANDELLS *stares, at him, then at* ANNE.)

ANNE: I told him.

WILL: What I find unbelievable is not what you do but what you all say, as if there's no angel in heaven writing it down, do you think so?

SANDELLS: Anne, I—

WILL: You lick away all night in some adulterous crotch and all day sing hymns to each other, as absent-minded as monkeys who eat their own excrement—

(SANDELLS *goes for his throat;* ANNE *runs to intervene, pulling and crying out and kicking at* SANDELLS.)

ANNE: Stop, stop, let go, ye—Berry! Berry!

(BERRY *runs in, and throws* SANDELLS *back: he stands, breathing, while* ANNE *cares for* WILL.)

Ye all right, lad?

(SANDELLS *takes a step to* ANNE.)

SANDELLS: I'm sorry, Anne, he—

ANNE [WHEELS]: Get out, get away from me, get, get—

(SANDELLS *falls back, shakes a finger at* WILL, *turns, goes off.*)

BERRY: Why don't ye keep ye tongue still?
WILL: It's the one thing I have loose.

(ANNE *sits, contemplates him;* BERRY *drifts off.*)

Anne, I know we must talk, and this isn't the place—
ANNE: It's the only place ye are.

(*Thumbs* SUSANNA.)

Get home.

(SUSANNA *backs off, wide-eyed.*)

WILL: I'm here with—
ANNE: They're nothing to me.
FULK: Thank ye.
WILL: Very well. I didn't take her there last night.
ANNE: Go on.
WILL: I didn't invite her, I didn't touch her, I didn't intend to, and I expect you to believe me.
ANNE [A PAUSE]: I'm glad, I didn't like to think ye ran from me to her. But I was upstairs afterwards waiting like a fool and ye ran out to this scum, why?
FULK: Thank ye. I haven't been so—
WILL: Fulk, the conversation is private.

FULK: Should I leave?

ANNE: Keep yc mouth shut. Ye wanted this to happen.

WILL: Partly—

ANNE: To get out of what ye promised?

WILL: —and partly not.

ANNE: Ye turned everything we said upside down—

WILL: Anne, it turned like a tide, I went out with it! I
never had more loving intentions—

FULK: He turned over a new leaf, it was the same on
both sides.

self why so much of me is treacheries.

WILL: —and since midnight here I've been asking my-

ANNE: And what did ye answer?

WILL: That I'm ignorant of what's in me, some—frac-
ture, I was half out of my head last night and
frantic to know which was my better half, sanity
or hallucination. You, the children, love, work,
honest sleep, that half is sanity—

ANNE: At least ye say it.

(KEMP *and* POPE *enter opposite to set up a money-
table and banners;* KEMP *approaches.*)

KEMP: Hideous sight, it unnerves me.

WILL: And the other half is hallucination.

ANNE: Will ye say what ye mean?

WILL: To be one of—them.

(ANNE's *eye follows his to* KEMP.)

KEMP [PAINED]: Lad, lad.

ANNE: Oh, God keep us.

WILL: Anne, I'm in pain, I can't think straight, but there's a question here of obedience, to others or myself. Obey and be stillborn—

ANNE: Can ye talk sense?

WILL: —but the disobedience in me—could obey them—

ANNE: I'm asking one thing—

WILL: —if they'd take me.

KEMP: Don't.

ANNE: I'm asking how are we to live!

WILL: And what am I asking? Damn you, damn you—

KEMP: Why?

WILL: —wear your work like—silk, you jigging doll, when the world wears rags—

KEMP: Silk?

WILL: What gives you the right, what? You stroll the countryside as carefree as a chickadee, chirping your ditties while others dig in the fields, you dazzle us with these banners of enchanted lands and when we're sick in our gut for them, where are you? Jigging away over the hilltop, leaving us tied, hobbled, chained, fettered, and locked in this stocks called life and love and family and—

(*He yanks at the stocks, yanks and yanks, heaving.*)

RICHARDS: Eh, eh!

FULK: He's daft.

WILL: Won't—no, get me—out—Berry! Berry! Get—
  me—

(*He stops, hangs in exhaustion.*)

FULK: Don't do that, boy.

(ANNE *comes to him, places a palm on his brow.*)

WILL [WEARY]: I'm not delirious now.

KEMP [QUIETLY]: Will you be out for the play?

WILL: Go away, you—fool's light—

(KEMP *bows, leaves with* POPE.)

ANNE: It's how ye—really feel about us, isn't it.

WILL: I have it in me to kill, yes. Or daydream it.

ANNE: Who now?

WILL: Women and children first.

ANNE: Susie?

WILL: Anne, it's only—

ANNE: Ye think, she'll die first too?

WILL: Yes. It's only the wishes—

ANNE: So ye can be with—strangers? these jigging—
  what did ye say, dolls, instead of the babes ye made
  in me—

WILL: —wishes on the night side of the eye—

ANNE: —and I screamed to get them out of my bones
  alive, ye own flesh, and—beauties, ye think if
  they're dead ye can be off with these make-believe

kings and dolls instead? Sweet, I'll give ye the chance!

(*She brings the bulky sack to the stocks, drops it.*)

WILL: What is it?
ANNE: It's ye things. I'm putting ye out of the house.
WILL: What?
ANNE: Ye can go where ye like, with these mudlarks or anywhere, do what ye like, lay with anyone—
WILL: It's my house.
ANNE: No. I talked it over with Gilbert, he helped me fill it.
WILL: Anne, this is the silliest thing you—
ANNE: I won't live with ye. No.
WILL: I'll carry it home again, that's—
ANNE: Then I'll take the children and go.

(WILL *stares.*)

Ye needn't kill us off, I won't share bed and board if ye can't want me the way—some of the way I want ye, and love ye—
WILL: I do—
ANNE: —because to have ye is what I wanted most, with all the worry ye were too much for me, and God knows there's little I wouldn't do for ye, only —there's nothing ye will do, to have me, and I'm not to be had for nothing.
WILL: I do, Anne, don't force a—

ANNE: No. If ye carry it home again it'll be to tell me
ye want us, ye'll work for us, ye'll live how people
who love each other live, for one another, and if
ye can't—if ye can't say it—

WILL: It's what I said and unsaid—

ANNE [UNSTEADY]: —don't come—

WILL: Love, I—can't—

ANNE: —please. Don't—come—

WILL: I can't say it!

(ANNE *stands, then hurries out; a silence.*)

FULK: Women. Think only of themselves, there's Meg
off with Kemp all night, saying prayers for me?

RICHARDS: What?

(*Opposite* SIR THOMAS *in somber mood and* BERRY
enter.)

FULK: Is our time up, pray God?

SIR THOMAS: Open the stocks. In the future, Richards,
you will not ignore my wishes.

RICHARDS: Was an oversight.

SIR THOMAS: I pray so. As for you two huntsmen, this
penalty might well have been uglier: I almost regret it was not. I have come from a—Kindly look
at me!

(WILL *raises his head.*)

It is your profligacies that others pay for, and you are heedless?

WILL: I pay.

SIR THOMAS: I would it were none but you: do you think you inhabit a void?

WILL: I—now do—

SIR THOMAS: It angers me how lightheaded you people are, not that I look to morality in you, but simple experience. I have just come from the girl you were with, whose life will be a tragedy, in exchange for an evening's lark. Are you ineducable as the bees that drown in the cider? tipplers, sluts, thieves, you—Are not worth the breath I waste.

(BERRY *has opened the stocks;* FULK *and* RICHARDS *crawl out, crooked, like paralytics on the ground. Opposite,* ROCHE *hurries in, sees* SIR THOMAS.)

ROCHE: Oh!

(*He turns to flee;* SIR THOMAS *spies him.*)

SIR THOMAS: Ah, Walter. I was expecting you. You left me a letter.

WILL: Why a tragedy?

ROCHE: You—read it, Sir Thomas?

SIR THOMAS: No.

ROCHE: I shall go at once for it, some—alterations—

SIR THOMAS: I have it here.

WILL: What tragedy?

SIR THOMAS [TURNS]: She will lose that foot, the surgeon
     is with her.

(*A silence.*)

WILL [STRICKEN]: What?

SIR THOMAS: Thanks to your—amorous attentions.

ROCHE: Oh, dear God.

SIR THOMAS [OPENS THE LETTER]: Walter, to happier
     matters. I take it your protégé is the—

ROCHE [TAKES IT]: No, no, my handwriting is illegible,
     perhaps I—

WILL: For a deer?

SIR THOMAS [TAKES IT BACK]: But I admire your script—

WILL: An eye for an eye, a foot for a deer?

ROCHE: I must explain that—circumstances, circum-
     stances—

WILL [SAVAGE]: You said morality?

ROCHE: —alter cases—

SIR THOMAS [STARES]: I said, your amorous attentions.
     It was not my lust that brought her there.

(WILL *covers his eyes with a hand.*)

ROCHE [TAKES THE LETTER]: My point is, certain changes
     —you may think advisable—

SIR THOMAS [TAKES IT BACK]: I am glad to advise.

ROCHE: No, my point is—

SIR THOMAS: It opens well, ablest young, yes, well quali-
     fied—

ROCHE: It continues in the same vein, I shall—
SIR THOMAS: What!

(*He stares at it, then wheels;* WILL *is weeping.*)

You? Is this a hoax, Walter?
ROCHE: Yes, I mean no, that was my point, I—
SIR THOMAS: You wrote this—perjured testimonial for
    a—
ROCHE: —before last night, Sir Thomas—
SIR THOMAS: And he turned scoundrel in the night?

(*He confronts* WILL.)

My ablest young—debaucher. It baffles me how
you arrived at the view that you, you, are fit to
teach the young. You will of course not, in Red-
ditch or elsewhere—
WILL: I set no trap for her.
SIR THOMAS: What?
WILL: Whatever else I did, I set no trap—
SIR THOMAS: Nor did I! And to involve my name now
    in this fraudulent letter—however you duped this
    old man—
WILL: The letter is of no interest to me, it never was.
ROCHE [WOUNDED]: Will.
WILL: That forlorn girl, so—vain of her looks, too—

(*At* RICHARDS.)

Why, you shit, why?

RICHARDS: Was an oversight!

SIR THOMAS: Spare us at least your obscenities.

WILL: You amputate our flesh, and speak of my obscenities?

SIR THOMAS: What!

(*He strikes his stick down upon the stocks;* WILL
recoils.)

You mistake my patience, I conquer it when necessary. Now heed me. If you violate law, property,
custom, and live by disobedience to the order of
things, do not have the presumption to ask why
suffering follows: it follows you.

WILL: Into whose trap?

SIR THOMAS: It was not my doing!

WILL: Not that it matters to her—

SIR THOMAS: The sole responsibility I accept for this
unhappy event is to see that henceforth you have
less margin for your floutings: little of what you
do will escape my attention, and the consequences
of the next folly will be dire. A word to the—

(*He holds up the letter, crumples and throws it.*)

—wise. Now, Walter.

ROCHE: I must explain, Sir Thomas, it was never my
intention to deceive you—

(ROCHE *trots after* SIR THOMAS *and* BERRY, *out;*
RICHARDS *limps out after them.* WILL *stumbles from
the stocks.*)

FULK: That's no good news. No. It's not good news—
WILL: Don't waste a tear, she's only a—drowned bee.
With one wish she'll—never get now—

(*He spies the sack.*)

Or—I.

(*He kneels to it, pulls out a fistful of garments.*)

She was here?
FULK: Who?
WILL: Talk sense, live how people live, she said it too,
what sense? Obey, obey—

(*He cries after* SIR THOMAS, *then after* ANNE.)

I'm living in a house of mad parents, everyone
tells me be one of the children, and I'm mad
enough myself to want their love and respect?

(*Presently he snatches up the letter, sits, digs a
stub out of his pocket, and writes on the back
side.*)

FULK: What are ye writing, another letter?

WILL: No.

FULK [PEERING]: It rhymes.

WILL: Luck.

FULK: First letter I've seen that rhymes.

WILL: It's not a letter, it's a defecation of principles.

FULK: Oh?

(*He reads as* WILL *writes.*)

The squire is dire, his sneer and his snare
Both stink up the air: his soul is a hole
Full of gases and prayer.

WILL: To John O'Green.

(*He gives the tune.*)

He thinks we're the dung—

FULK [SINGS]: *—that he saunters among,*
It's himself that he smells and tastes on his tongue.
Ho, that's very good, who's this letter to?

WILL: It rhymes, therefore it's a poem. Find me a nail
or a sliver.

(FULK *searches on the ground,* WILL *scribbles.*)

FULK: Here, what's it for?

(WILL *takes it, tacks the page up on the stocks*
post.)

Somehow I feel I'm getting guilty again—

WILL: Name me a bad dog, they get bad doggerel, but
it has much authentic feeling in it.

FULK: It's a beautiful sentiment. Only are ye sure ye
should put it up?

WILL: Yes and no—

(*He pauses.*)

—why not, if it's all or nothing let it be nothing.

(TWO TOWNSMEN *enter in conversation; they stare
at* WILL *reading, and he beckons them over, to read
at his shoulder.*)

TOWNSMAN: Haw. Sir Thomas.

WILL [GIVES THE TUNE]:
The folk are a-choke, the law is his stick—

TOWNSMEN [JOINING IN]:
*His power is sour, his people are sick
Of so upright a prick!*

TOWNSMAN [CONVULSED]: Haw, who put it up here?

FULK: Richards.

(*Townsfolk gather around the page, and sing;
others come on.* WILL *looks off.*)

WILL: Fulk, let's spread the bad word of shit, piss, and
corruption.

FULK: Where?

WILL: Everywhere, the town is full of it.

(*He and* FULK *go quickly off, as* SIR THOMAS *returns with* RICHARDS *and* BERRY; *the* TOWNSPEOPLE *sing on.*)

SIR THOMAS: You say Kemp?

RICHARDS: I think he was one.

SIR THOMAS: This player Kemp? He would not—

(*The* TOWNSPEOPLE *become silent.*)

He would not risk the license here of his company—

RICHARDS: It was something they said.

SIR THOMAS: Fetch him, Berry.

(BERRY *runs to obey;* SIR THOMAS *sees a* VERY OLD MAN *peering at the stocks, approaches behind him, reads.*)

VERY OLD MAN: Heh.

(*He turns.*)

Heh, heee—

(*He retreats in consternation.*)

sir thomas: Come here.

(*The* very old man *halts.*)

Who put this up?
very old man: Eh, I'm an—old man.
sir thomas: I asked who put it up.
very old man: Couldn't—say.

(sir thomas *gazes around at the* townspeople.)

sir thomas: Who wrote this?
townswoman: I—only heard, Sir Thomas—
sir thomas: I asked who.
townswoman: —by hearsay—
sir thomas: Who?
townswoman: Richards.
richards [dizzily]: What?
townswoman: So they say—
sir thomas: Richards?

(*He plucks the page loose, turns it over, stares;*
berry *returns with* kemp.)

richards: Who says?
townsman: Everybody says.
townswoman: My brother saw ye.
fulk [in the crowd]: It's back in the stocks for ye,
    Richards!
sir thomas: Bring me that man.

(BERRY *brings* FULK *to him, struggling.*)

RICHARDS: Sir Thomas, Sir Thomas, believe me, there's
    some mistake, how can anyone say—
SIR THOMAS: Be quiet: you are innocent and incapable.
    Kemp. Did you accompany him last night?
KEMP: No. Who is he?
SIR THOMAS: Did he not accompany you?
FULK: No, who is he?

(SIR THOMAS *contemplates* KEMP, *then* FULK.)

SIR THOMAS: Berry, take this ragbag to the whipping
    post. See if the truth is in him.
FULK [PANICKY]: Sir, ye wouldn't whip an old soldier
    who—

(BERRY *thrusts him toward the stocks post.*)

—gave his arm for the Queen—
WILL [IN THE CROWD]: Why him? Be dire and whip the
    Earl of Leicester's man.
SIR THOMAS: What?

(A FEW TOWNSPEOPLE *melt away from* WILL, SIR
THOMAS *sees him.*)

Ah.
KEMP: Me, you brat?

WILL: Oh, of course not. You travel under the Earl's protection—

KEMP: I do, and neither of us likes to see me whipped.

WILL: —and justice here is judicious, it has a cautious taste for cripples.

KEMP [THEN]: Don't, lad.

SIR THOMAS: You are friends?

KEMP: I like the boy, yes.

SIR THOMAS: Berry. I think we will set this old soldier free—

FULK [DUCKS AWAY]: Thank ye.

SIR THOMAS [WITH THE PAGE]: —in favor of our young poet. I take it this side is the fruit of the long studies for which Master Roche commends you, on the other?

WILL: Is your question did I write it?

SIR THOMAS: Yes.

WILL: Of course.

SIR THOMAS: Your candor is encouraging. Now, was this player with you last night?

WILL: I think I wrote it in vain.

SIR THOMAS: Will you answer the question?

WILL: With all candor. You mutilate one of us for life, put three of us in the stocks, keep the rest of us from a heroic play while you order a cowardly whipping, and all for the sake of one louse-bitten deer: a town that turns on such a question is crackbrained.

(A silence.)

KEMP: Now, now. I'll pay for the damned deer, we can get on with the play—

SIR THOMAS: I have underestimated you. Bind him to the post.

(BERRY *thrusts* WILL *to the post.*)

KEMP: What, are you going to whip the boy?

SIR THOMAS: The decision is not mine. Were you with him or not?

(KEMP *hesitates.*)

Do, Berry.

KEMP: I was with him.

SIR THOMAS: Honor, among thieves. It is inspiring to find it even there. You and your company will return to your rooms, and wait.

POPE: We're giving a play.

SIR THOMAS: Obviously there will be no play.

TOWNSMAN: No play?

TOWNSWOMAN: Sir Thomas, let's have the play—

KEMP: You deprive us of our livelihood.

NED: Willie, be quiet.

KEMP: Why?

NED: You're in the wrong.

TOWNSMAN [CALLING]: Give us the play—

SIR THOMAS: Take your money home again: you have greater needs than for their shams. You will go to your rooms.

KEMP: Then turn the boy loose.

SIR THOMAS: Ah yes, the boy.

(He considers the page, the watching crowd, WILL at the post with BERRY.)

The law has a body, however invisible to you, it is all that guards us from each other. In this town I personify it.

WILL: Oh, the obscenities of office, the law is in your hands, isn't it your hand my jingle burns?

SIR THOMAS: It is not the private offense that concerns me—

WILL: I know, the aloof arbiter, I prefer the honor of thieves—

SIR THOMAS: I will have obedience to authority here as I give it to authority—

WILL: And by what authority is it you rule us in every step we—

SIR THOMAS: By that with which I rule myself.

WILL: Liar!

(A buzz in the crowd.)

SIR THOMAS: I said I rule myself, my passions, and my judg—

WILL: Liar! Your passion is rule, and it rules you. You herd us into the dark under your hand and create a town you despise—

SIR THOMAS: Nine lashes, Berry! One to the line. Go to
your rooms and wait.

(*He starts off. The* TOWNSPEOPLE *stir, muttering.*)

TOWNSMAN: Let them give the play, Sir Thomas.

TOWNSWOMAN: Yes, let's have the play.

TOWNSMAN: Give us the play.

SIR THOMAS [TURNS]: There will be no play, I have re-
voked it. You have a whipping to divert you.

TOWNSMAN: We want the play.

TOWNSWOMAN: Let's have the play.

SIR THOMAS: Go to your homes and your work. You
but waste good time and money on these—

(*The mutter grows to a chant.*)

TOWNSPEOPLE: Let's have the play. Let's have the play.
Let's have the play.

WILL: *The folk are a-choke—*

TOWNSMAN: *—the law is his stick—*

SIR THOMAS: I say go to your work!

(*Others take up the song, with laughter.*)

TOWNSPEOPLE: *His power is sour, his people are sick*
Of so upright a prick—

SIR THOMAS: Your ballad monger shall bear the—

(*The singing drowns him out; at the first break he calls across.*)

Ten lashes, Berry.

(*They sing on, jeering, until another break.*)

Twelve lashes!

(*They sing on, uglier.*)

Fifteen lashes!
KEMP: Damn you, stop singing it!

(*Out of the crowd a raw egg is thrown, strikes* SIR THOMAS *on the breast, and trickles down. The singing straggles out.* SIR THOMAS *stands rigid; the crowd is uneasy under his glare.*)

SIR THOMAS [AT LAST]: What are you all? angry as apes and frightened as deer, louts, lechers, mud men—

(*They avoid his eyes, here, there.*)

Are you teachable only by the most drastic of punishments? Then we shall have that lesson too. Tell the bailiff to call the council in session. Now.

(RICHARDS *runs out;* SIR THOMAS *turns on* WILL.)

You infect all. Fifteen lashes, Berry, and when you
are done bring him to the Gild Hall. With his
friends.

KEMP: For what?

SIR THOMAS: For bloodletting, to cure these—children
of their fever.

(*He goes off.*)

TOWNSMAN [SPITS]: No play.

TOWNSMAN: Well, let's watch the whipping.

(BERRY *takes up the whip; the* TOWNSPEOPLE
gather.)

WILL: Instead. Get on with the bloodletting, you
damned geese, you—moment ago were quacking
what I put in your mouths, now you—

(*Some jeer in his face; he breaks one hand loose
to swing, but they pin him to the post, and bind
him again.*)

—he's right, worse than children—no wit to invent
your own rhyme—

(*They jeer him down, he shouts over, and* BERRY
heaves the whip back.)

—or dare mouth it except behind each other, geese, geese, a flock of idiot—aaahh—

(*The lash tears the cry from him; he grips the post. Silence. The lights begin to dim out;* BERRY *heaves the whip back, and lashes with it again, and again, and again.*)

END OF THE ACT

ACT III

———

Adversity,
Which, like the toad, ugly and venomous,
Wears yet a precious jewel in his head.

SCENE 1

FAINT LIGHT STEALING IN ON A FEW BENCHES IN ROWS, FACING A TABLE; IT DARKENS AS TIME PASSES.

WILL IS SEATED ON THE FLOOR, HIS ARMS AND HEAD DOWN UPON A BENCH, NOT STIRRING; HIS SHIRT IS BLOODY AND IN SHREDS. AT THE TABLE SIR THOMAS SITS, ALSO MOTIONLESS, STARING AT HIM.

SIR THOMAS: Are you awake?

(WILL *continues to lie with eyes closed;* SIR THOMAS *continues to sit, pondering.*)

I know of no other way.

(A *mutter of voices, off;* BERRY *pushes* KEMP *in.*)

KEMP: Careful—
BERRY: Sir Thomas, the one without the arm has a whore, ye want to talk to her?
SIR THOMAS: No. I will.

(*He rises, walks past* KEMP *and out;* BERRY *follows.*
KEMP *looks around.*)

KEMP: You asleep, lad?

WILL [UNMOVING]: Yes.

KEMP: Don't let me wake you.

WILL: You did.

KEMP: I've been in jollier holes of justice than this.

WILL: You did. I don't know whether to thank or damn
    you for a devil.

KEMP: What?

WILL: Take me up on a mountain and show me the
    cities of the world—

KEMP: Oh.

WILL: —a view worth being whipped for? Without it I
    had a—

(*He sits up, grits his teeth;* KEMP *squats to examine
his back.*)

—family, a trade, and a whole skin.

KEMP: Well, you talked him into it.

WILL: Yes, he's—putty in my hands.

KEMP: You'll live.

WILL [PRESENTLY]: Where?

(KEMP *sits on a bench, considers him.*)

And for whom? If not for them.

KEMP: Don't ask me.

WILL: Some—halfwit foetus in me bleating for—more life?

KEMP: Damn it, I'm not the father. I came into town to make a living, not show you anything.

(*He walks away, walks back.*)

Look, you want to go to London, go.

WILL: I don't need your consent.

KEMP: Good.

WILL: I need Sir Thomas's.

KEMP: Just get it out of your head we're taking you. I like your company, my—company likes its own, half the time we don't keep our ass above water, what can you do for us, sell sausages in the pit? You want my advice?

WILL: Not so far.

KEMP: Make your peace with him, and stay.

WILL: It's with a different enemy.

KEMP: Your wife, then.

WILL: Myself.

KEMP: Cities of the world, my God, these mudpuddle towns, work, worry, sleep in ditches, miss meals, miss women, your clothes stink—It's a wormy dog's life, with always some blacksuit bastard like his holiness to kick us, and here's a—

(*He comes back, sits.*)

—lovely town, you do a day's work, you have a roof and a woman cooking and your brats to wel-

come you home of a winter evening. Know what
any of us would give for that?

WILL: Not two pins.

KEMP: One.

WILL: What can his holiness do to you?

KEMP: Run us out, that's all, won't be the first time.
What can he do to you?

WILL: Anything he likes. And that's a difference.

(*A mutter of voices, off.*)

BERRY [OFF]: —be a while yet. In there.
(ANNE *walks in.*)

KEMP: Well, speak of the—Mouse herself.

(ANNE *spies* WILL, *catches her breath.*)

I'll wait.

(*He goes out;* WILL *stands, sways.*)

WILL: Whipped me.

ANNE: Oh my God, ye're all—blood—

(*She blunders around a bench to him; he tries to
forestall her with a hand.*)

WILL: Hands—off, no, no, don't—

(ANNE *takes his hand to her bosom, and he is sud-
denly undone; she sits, he goes to his knees with*

his head into her lap, but fighting off tears, striking the bench.)

ANNE: What is it, what is it?
WILL: I'm afraid, I'm afraid—
ANNE: Don't. Lad, lad.

(She lulls him in her lap.)

There. Don't. There.
WILL: I wrote a verse. To which he—was averse—

(She touches him inadvertently.)

Aa—
ANNE: Get the shirt off, I'll find—
WILL: Don't move.
ANNE: —some water, dirt's all in it, ye'll be sick with—
WILL: Don't move. Oh God, it's good to touch you.
ANNE: Do, do.
WILL: I could melt into you, I never felt so cut off from —all other flesh in my—

(He rolls away from her.)

Oh, damn you, damn the—
ANNE: What did I—
WILL: —smell and taste of you, nothing's wrong the minute I'm in your arms, you great bitch, why?

(He is on his feet, unsteady; ANNE eyes him.)

ANNE [DRY]: Ye love me. Maybe.

WILL: I won't keep any promise I make, do you hear
me?

ANNE: The whole town hears ye.

(*She rises, crosses back;* WILL *sits on a bench.*)

WILL: I won't melt into you, no, that's one I'll keep.

ANNE [HALF OFF]: I want some water and soap and
clean rags.

BERRY [HALF IN]: What for?

ANNE: For him, ye think I'm doing ye floor? Get them.

(BERRY *retreats;* ANNE *comes back, starts to slip the
shirt off.*)

WILL: Slow.

(ANNE *gets it off, stares, swallows, sits, and stares.*)

ANNE: Ye're a rare-looking schoolmaster—

WILL: It's skin deep.

ANNE: What's next, husband pet?

WILL: I mean nothing's changed.

ANNE [THEN]: I know. Did he say what he wants ye
here for?

WILL: Said bloodletting, since I still have some, but
what he'll do I—Banish me from the town?

(ANNE's *eyes widen, she gets up.*)

ANNE: He said that?

WILL: Kemp expects it. Let him, it isn't the garden of
Eden even if He puts me out of it.

ANNE: If he does—that, I can't let that—

(BERRY *appears with a bucket and rags.* ANNE *walks,
takes them;* BERRY *gapes at* WILL's *back, she glares.*)

Ye like it?

BERRY: I do—what I'm told—

ANNE: Then get me a shirt. Ye didn't have the sense to
take it off?

(BERRY *retreats.* ANNE *kneels behind* WILL, *cleans
dirt from the wounds; he is gritty with the pain.*)

WILL: Easy.

ANNE: Hold still, it's hard enough. Ye—want him to?

WILL: It's too hard. What?

ANNE: Drive ye out?

WILL: I don't need his consent, do I?

ANNE: Go with these gipsies ye love so?

WILL: They—aa—

(*He sucks in, arching.*)

Talk of—someone you like better—

ANNE: I can't help it.

WILL: They don't want me either.

ANNE [A PAUSE]: Ah.

(*She puts her brow against his shoulder.*)

They can't have ye.

WILL: Anne, Anne. Wasn't the whipping, it was the terror at—being spat out, like a gob of gristle. So unwanted—

(*She kisses his bare shoulder.*)

—they watched me like a ring of mongrels—

ANNE: I like ye gristle—

WILL: To be different from them is to die, that was the terror. I wanted to crawl home to—you, her, some womb—and couldn't, cut off there too—

ANNE: Don't.

(*She turns his cheek, his body comes toward her.*)

WILL: No, don't kiss me, I taste of vomit—

(*She kisses him; and his hands gather her head, a long hungering kiss. At last she sits back.*)

Will you love, honor, and live with—my vomit?

ANNE: No.

WILL: Then what are we to do?

(ANNE *shakes her head.*)

If we first met now we'd see each other so—simply, I'd say there's an uncommon lass, I'll marry you.

ANNE: I'd say good, I've three children I think are yours.
WILL: I'd say—I love you, nothing's wrong, I love you.

(ANNE *shuts her eyes on it.*)

And you'd say yes, live how people who love one
another—
ANNE: I know what I said.

(A *pause.*)

I'll give ye—time.
WILL [SHAKY]: Anne, I love you, nothing's not wrong,
I love you, it's—cracking me apart—

(ANNE *takes his hand; they sit, mute.*)

ANNE: Then we'll work it out. Whatever he does.

(*The tolling of a bell begins its summons. In a
moment* BERRY *prods* FULK *in, with* MEG, *and
tosses* ANNE *the sack of* WILL's *things, from which
she takes a shirt;* KEMP *appears, and townspeople,
including* GILBERT *with* SUSANNA—*she runs to* WILL
—*and* SANDELLS, *the players,* HODGES, *a growing
throng.* BERRY *lights tapers, and the lights come
up; he seats* KEMP, FULK, *and* MEG *on a bench in
front. The tolling dies away.* SIR THOMAS *enters,
pauses in a momentary contemplation of* WILL
with SUSANNA.)

SIR THOMAS: Be seated there, please.

(WILL *sits beside* KEMP. ANNE *takes* SUSANNA *back,
and sits;* ROCHE, RICHARDS, *others stand at the rear;
when* SIR THOMAS *lays his stick and papers on the
table, and sits to them, the room becomes hushed.*)

I have the council's consent to proceed in this
matter as I deem necessary. The events of this
afternoon are or should be of concern to all of us.
I need only—

(KEMP *whispers to* WILL.)

I should like to have your attention, Kemp.
KEMP: Sorry.
SIR THOMAS: You believe that a minor notoriety as a
clown exempts you from our provincial law?
KEMP: I'm sorry. I did say I'm—
WILL: Kemp, our state of mind is irrelevant here—

(A *stir.*)

SIR THOMAS: Mine is not. I have little appetite for what
I must do to make an example of you, kindly do
not aggravate it.

(*To* KEMP)

You do not retract your admission of poaching?

KEMP: Only my offer to pay for it. Our pockets are empty, thanks.

SIR THOMAS: We shall find another means.

(*To* FULK)

This woman is your wife?

FULK: No, sir.

MEG [WITH HIM]: Yes, sir.

FULK: In a manner of speaking.

SIR THOMAS: In a manner of fornication. What is your means of support?

FULK: A bit of—fishing, hunting—

SIR THOMAS: Thieving. I am told you also sell your lady's charms.

FULK: Who, me?

MEG: No, sir.

SIR THOMAS: You have not whored under the hedges repeatedly?

MEG: No, sir, no—

SIR THOMAS: I have a tally of townsmen here with whom you have been seen on divers occasions, must I read it?

(A *buzz.*)

I think if you both acknowledge this—dark past,

your future will be brighter.

FULK: Well. Maybe on—some divers occasions—

SIR THOMAS: Thank you.

(*To* WILL)

Now. You are one and twenty?

WILL: Older, since yesterday.

SIR THOMAS: This is your child.

(WILL *turns his head, to gaze at* SUSANNA.)

WILL: Mine.

ANNE [UP]: We have twins at home, Sir Thomas—

SUSANNA: No, we don't.

ANNE: We have twins.

SIR THOMAS: As a plea for clemency they would have
    been twice as eloquent.

WILL: The child is not my plea.

ANNE: She came unasked—

SIR THOMAS: It is not important. How long are you
    married?

WILL: Why do you catechize me, come to whatever
    decision—

ANNE: Four years.

SIR THOMAS: How old are you, child?

SUSANNA: Four years.

(*Some snickering.*)

WILL [TERSE]: You outwit children, sir?

SIR THOMAS [PRESENTLY]: You are intelligent: would it
    not be intelligent to keep in mind the realities of
    local power?

WILL: It has crossed my—back—

SIR THOMAS: And be—in so public a place—contrite?

WILL [A PAUSE]: Ah, is that what you ask?

SIR THOMAS: I shall help you. Sandells, you were sponsor
    of this couple at their marriage, tell me—

SANDELLS: Ye're making a show of the wife. It's not
    right.

SIR THOMAS: No. I wish to learn solely your—

ANNE: There's nothing to learn but what every donkey
    in town's been braying for four years. It was my
    doing.

WILL [TENSE]: Anne, I want you quiet here.

(ANNE *sits.*)

SIR THOMAS: —solely your impression of his character.

SANDELLS: I was—partial in the matter, I didn't know
    him too well. Then.

HODGES [UP]: I know him too well, I've had trouble with
    him before this. I don't mean to talk out of my
    turn—

SIR THOMAS: Continue.

HODGES: Well, there's my girl in her room, won't—walk

again, no, what am I to do with her now? a lass
who's a—dragging cripple the rest of her life, who'll
want her? and whose fault is it?

WILL: Mine, hers, yours, his—

HODGES: Hers!

WILL: —and the trap's.

HODGES: She wouldn't have been there without ye!

SIR THOMAS: Nor would the trap.

SANDELLS: It's true he was never anything but bad luck
to anyone.

HODGES: The sooner the town's rid of him the better off
it'll be, I say get rid of him!

(WILL *rises in a hubbub of hostile voices; he gazes
around, shaken.* ROCHE *stands, uncertain.*)

ROCHE: Sir Thomas.

SIR THOMAS: Yes.

ROCHE: I too have been disturbed by today's events. Yet
the youth is my friend. I wonder—

TOWNSMAN: Ye need a new friend or we need a new
schoolmaster!

ROCHE [RATTLED]: —wonder whether we—do not perhaps overlook a consideration? I mean that the
intelligence of which you spoke, the abilities with
which I am acquainted in this—

SANDELLS: What abilities?

RICHARDS: Writing songs against ye and blaming them
on me?

HODGES: And who taught him that?

SIR THOMAS: It is an interesting point, Walter, whether
education does not unlock a Pandora's box of vices
upon us?

ROCHE: Well. I am—not the one to—

WILL: You forget, perhaps, the last vice that flew out
of her box.

SIR THOMAS: What?

WILL: Hope.

SIR THOMAS [PRESENTLY]: You are not without interest.
I bear it in mind, Walter: it is what makes him
contagious.

(*He studies the crowd.*)

A town is a pond from which all must drink: when
it turns unclean, the health of all requires that its
scum be cleared. In public view.

(*A silence; he turns to the four.*)

Kemp, the disturbance today arose in good part
from the presence here of you and your strollers:
they will leave the town within the hour.

KEMP: What, be on the road in the dark?

SIR THOMAS: And you for your personal exploit will be
whipped out.

(*A buzz.*)

KEMP: What?

SIR THOMAS: Whipped out.

KEMP: I'm here under the warrant of the—

SIR THOMAS: A letter will go to the Earl of Leicester.

KEMP: He's leading an army, he can't be thinking of trivia!

SIR THOMAS: It will be an unfortunate army. Sit.

KEMP: I'm—

SIR THOMAS: And be silent!

(KEMP *slowly obeys.*)

You two vagabonds, it is clear, are habituated to being plague spots. Berry, the whore is also to be whipped out.

MEG [WHIMPERS]: No, no—

SIR THOMAS: This fetid pimp no doubt has seen the bloody heads of thieves and such malefactors stuck on the gate pikes of more than one city: you know the penalties?

FULK [WETS HIS LIPS]: Yes, sir.

SIR THOMAS: I shall not exact them to the full. You will suffer the severance of one hand.

FULK: One—one—

(*The room is chilled;* FULK *begins to weep.*)

SIR THOMAS: Now, my bird of paradise, what shall I do with you, have your tongue removed?

(WILL *stares at him, dumb;* ANNE *soon rises in agitation.*)

ANNE: Sir Thomas, sir, I—Can I speak a—word—
SIR THOMAS: In his stead? No.

(*A wait.*)

He seems quite tongueless now.
WILL [BLANCHED]: Do you—do you—
ANNE: Please—
WILL: —dare?
SIR THOMAS: You dare think not?
ANNE: Please, I'm not arguing what he's done, the right
    or wrong, but when he's wrong he grants it—
SIR THOMAS: I have not heard him grant it.
WILL: Anne—
ANNE: —but it's done, will cutting out his tongue give
    the girl a foot back? Or doing what Hodges says
    either, ye drive my lad out it won't help ye daugh-
    ter, it only hurts mine here, and isn't it ye own girl
    matters to ye? I'll make it up to ye myself, don't
    ask what ye asked and I'll—come do her work—
SIR THOMAS: The girl is not the issue.
WILL: No.
SIR THOMAS: But penitence is.

(*He waits on* WILL.)

I invite it.

(WILL *sits wordless; then* SIR THOMAS *slaps the table.*)

Berry, you will take this—

(WILL *stands up in a fear;* ANNE *cuts in.*)

ANNE: No! Now ye make a joke of the child being here, a plea for—whatever it was ye said, and why not? Ye're a learned man and I don't follow all ye words, but God hears—

(*She is fierce.*)

—what mouthfuls of nonsense men talk with big words, now I'll tell ye what's real in the world and it's not towns is ponds, it's the lad ye buried in the churchyard not so long ago, and when ye lady first heard him cry in her blood and gave suck to him she knew nothing was real or mattered but that he be kept alive, and kept safe, and if ye remember him ye'll know how I hurt for mine, hurt for mine—

(SIR THOMAS *is motionless.*)

And ye'll forgive me for my—my—
SIR THOMAS: Trespasses. Is an honored word. You say unreal, who is to so order the world that others

than yours may be kept safe? I am not simply
punishing the past.

ANNE [DESPERATE]: What do ye want of him?

SIR THOMAS: He knows.

ANNE [TURNS]: Then tell him.

(WILL *shakes his head.*)

He can't, he's afraid, can't ye see he's afraid of ye,
what more do ye need?

SIR THOMAS: To hear him say it. Is it true?

ANNE: Of course it's true, tell him, why do ye all put on
such faces? ye're ashamed he'll know? He said after
the whipping—

WILL: Stop—

ANNE: No, he's afraid is what he told me! All he wanted
was to crawl home, he told me that too. And not
to me only, to his mother, or any—

WILL [VIOLENT]: Stop it!

SIR THOMAS: Is it true? It will serve.

ANNE: Ye'd sooner lose a tongue than say it?

(WILL *on his feet to stare around sees* SUSANNA.)

For—us?

SIR THOMAS: I tell you this, say it now or you will say
nothing hereafter.

ANNE: Tell him it's true!

WILL [FINALLY]: It's—true, it's—true, true, I—

(*He closes his eyes, bending over to hide.*)

—won't, no, not—cry—

(*But he goes to his knees, and into his hands,
weeping. A silence, all watching.* ANNE *comes to
kneel at his side, he twists and crawls away from
her.*)

SIR THOMAS [SOON]: I am not oblivious to my memories.
They include his father, who long served the town,
and he himself is not without qualities which can
be useful here. He has learned a lesson, we see,
that Walter failed to teach him.
ROCHE [UNSTEADY]: Yes.
SIR THOMAS: Berry, as to this pair—
BERRY: Yes, sir.
SIR THOMAS: The penalties I spoke of will be executed
tomorrow at daybreak. Is it clear to all?

(*He surveys the room; all are still, or murmur as-
sent.*)

Until then, you are at liberty. To vanish.
FULK: Wha—what—
MEG: Go?
FULK: Ah, thank ye, sir, thank ye—

(*He endeavors to kiss* SIR THOMAS's *hand.*)

SIR THOMAS [IN DISTASTE]: Stop that.

> (*To the roomful*)

Very well, this hearing is at an end. You may now leave.

> (*The* TOWNSPEOPLE *stand, disperse in a buzz of voices, straggle out;* FULK *and* MEG *push out in a hurry.*)

KEMP: I'm included?
SIR THOMAS: You will most certainly be whipped out in one hour.

> (KEMP *turns and goes, the* PLAYERS *after him;* NED *lingers.*)

NED: My friend doesn't represent us in the best light. For myself, I—offer our apologies, and—

> (SIR THOMAS *ignores him;* NED *goes, with the last of the crowd.* WILL *lies against a bench, and* ANNE *comes back to him.* SIR THOMAS *signals her out; she retreats to* SUSANNA, *and they leave.* SIR THOMAS *contemplates* WILL, *alone in the room.*)

SIR THOMAS: May I counsel you?

(WILL *is silent. Presently* SIR THOMAS *gathers his papers and stick; he walks past him.*)

WILL [THEN]: I—regret the jingle, I wrote it in anger.

(SIR THOMAS *turns.*)

It does you some injustice.

SIR THOMAS: I had you whipped in anger. Justice should be—judicious.

WILL: I think you're quoting me. And when he took the whip to me I was quoting you about this herd of louts, that's a riddle, isn't it, that we'd be in such accord while you're flogging me?

SIR THOMAS: The defects in man's nature jump to the eye.

WILL: I think mine jump faster, to a whip. Or other threats. Yes.

SIR THOMAS: To banish you was my—expectation.

WILL: She thought only to save me.

SIR THOMAS: And did.

WILL: Yes. To be what, a continual—speck in your eye?

SIR THOMAS: I have other expectations. You have learned that in human affairs, unhappily, the exercise of authority is indispensable: bend to it.

WILL: Or break.

SIR THOMAS: Yes.

WILL: I—broke.

SIR THOMAS: Bend to it.

(*He turns, to leave.*)

WILL: No. The world isn't a—skull that says me nay,
     it's a godhead alive with tongues. Yours is but one.
     You asked who is to—order was your word—
SIR THOMAS: Yes.
WILL: And who is?
SIR THOMAS: Those who make order in themselves.
WILL: And how shall I make order of the—contrarieties
     in me?
SIR THOMAS: By giving up parts of yourself, as all men
     do: it is called self-mastery.
WILL [CAREFULLY]: Which parts?
SIR THOMAS: You have the precepts of a thousand years
     to instruct you.
WILL: Which is to say all wisdom is in, keep the box
     closed. Or open it up, heads, guts, hearts, see what
     we are? and perhaps at the bottom is hope. Of
     something else, something in us I—have no tongue
     for, hear flowing, underground, elusive as water,
     but compress it enough it will move stones to get
     out. What, are there no surprises in us?
SIR THOMAS: Fewer, as I age. You are one.

(*He returns, pinches out the candles; lights down.*)

The winter will be long, we may talk again.
WILL: With your half of it written on my back?
SIR THOMAS: I doubt it will be needed now. I wrote
     only make order in yourself.

WILL: It is my prayer.

(SIR THOMAS *walks out;* WILL *sits alone among the benches, with his sack, and the faint thud of the drum is heard.*)

SCENE 2

TWILIGHT; THE EMPTY STOCKS. THE DRUM IS DISTANT. WILL PUTS HIS SACK DOWN, RISES WITH JACKET IN HAND, GAZES ABOUT.

WILL: Gather, now gather all my cruelties into one scalpel and cry, to put off the skin of my past, though its blood like a birthmark taint me forever. Town, steeple, marketplace, the stones I learned to walk on, like the loves of a childhood now must dwindle behind me: before me, all is. Tooth and nail, of such is the kingdom, destroy or lie uncreated: and I will be, if I undo a world—

(SUSANNA *runs in to him.*)

SUSANNA: Papa—

(*He turns, and catches her up.*)

WILL: Bug, bug—
SUSANNA: Mommy said catch up with ye.

WILL [RACKED]: I can't, I can't, I can't—

(*He rocks with her in his arms. Opposite,* ANNE *hurries in.*)

ANNE: Will. I'm sorry for what I—did there, or said, I said only what someone had to—
WILL: Yes.
ANNE: For ye own sake, lad.
WILL: I know.
ANNE: And mine. And hers.
WILL: Yes. To keep what I have, I must—learn to obey—

(*The drum interrupts; the* PLAYERS *come in with their bundles to a dead march, and break up laughing.* HEMING *leaps on the stocks, where he addresses* SUSANNA.)

HEMING: Old faces and new friends. There's an old face—
NED [IMPATIENT]: Come along, come along.
HEMING: Do you believe in plays?
SUSANNA: Momma, I didn't see the play—

(*She runs crying to* ANNE, *who hugs her;* KEMP *hurries in.*)

ANNE: Now, now, there'll be others—
NED [MEANWHILE]: Save your strength. We've a long walk ahead, and no sleep.

KEMP: We'll put up under a hedge.

NED: I'm grateful to you. A brilliant engagement!

(*They straggle out with their bundles;* KEMP *remains.*)

KEMP: We're in a hurry. Give me the play you stole.

(*He points to* WILL'*s jacket;* WILL *lifts the text from a pocket,* KEMP *takes it.*)

Good luck, lad. If you're ever in London, look for me.

(KEMP *nods to* ANNE, *shoulders his bundle, and hurries after the others. The drum and trumpet are heard receding.*)

WILL: Kemp!

KEMP [TURNS]: Yes?

(WILL *hesitates on* ANNE *and* SUSANNA, *then is headlong.*)

WILL: I'll sell sausages in the pit.

KEMP: What?

WILL: Let me come.

KEMP: Where, London?

WILL: With you.

KEMP: Now?

WILL: Yes.

KEMP: You're daft.

WILL: Tell me come.

KEMP: You'd never walk it, a night in the stocks and a flogging—

WILL: I'll walk it.

KEMP: I know you're playstruck, give yourself a little time to ponder it, you'll—

WILL: Don't lecture me, say yes or no!

KEMP: No!

WILL: I'm coming.

ANNE: What?

KEMP: No! You think I'm daft too? Your name is trouble, boy—

WILL: I'm coming with you.

KEMP: No, you're not. I'd as soon have a hive of bees in my crotch as you in a company—

WILL: The road's free, I can walk where I please.

KEMP: Not with me.

WILL: I'll be with you at the bridge—

KEMP: We'll throw you in the river!

(KEMP *hurries out with his bundle.*)

WILL [SHOUTS]: I'm coming!

(*The drum recedes.* WILL *turns back to* ANNE, *and* SUSANNA *runs to him; he steps back, fending her off.*)

SUSANNA: Papa—

WILL: No. Get away. No.

ANNE: What crazy—ye said they—

SUSANNA: —I didn't see the play—

WILL: Take her home.

ANNE: Them, ye're going with—

WILL: Yes.

ANNE: —them, now? But none of us—Lad, we can't—

WILL: Alone.

ANNE: Alone!

SUSANNA [RUNS BACK]: Ye promised ye'd take me to the
    play—

ANNE: Be still!

*(She slaps SUSANNA, who falls back a step; ANNE
at once reaches for her, but SUSANNA twists free,
runs wailing to WILL, and he kneels to embrace
her.)*

WILL: Now listen, now listen, I'm in trouble here, bug,
    I'm—going away—

ANNE: How do ye mean alone?

WILL: —to a great city, full of so many things, I'll send
    you such—things—

ANNE: Answer me, what's alone?

WILL: —go hug Mommy, she loves you more than I
    do, she's a most—

(He turns SUSANNA back toward ANNE.)

—giving—

ANNE: How do ye mean alone?

WILL: I can't live with you. Not now, not—live—

(ANNE *holds* SUSANNA *to her skirt, rigid.*)

ANNE: Why?

WILL: —not obey, not obey—

ANNE: Ye mean here.

WILL: —not lose what piece of me is left—

ANNE: We'll come there.

WILL [TORN]: No. Not serve—

ANNE: What?

WILL: I can't—serve, him or you, till I'm all of a piece
   I can't—give, live for, love—

ANNE: Love—

WILL: —everything I love in you—

ANNE: Ye never did!

WILL: Half of me—

ANNE [FIERCE]: Do ye know what the word means?

WILL: —half of me was born in you, love, it means—
   you and he are one voice now, you said what he
   said, obey what is. Let me go—

(ANNE *stares at him; it is by an effort she says it.*)

ANNE: Ye're—leaving me, lad? Ye won't—send for us—

WILL: If I can.

ANNE: —or ever come back—

WILL [DESPERATE]: If I can! Not now, whatever I—uproot in the ribs of me—

(*He touches* SUSANNA's *head, a last time;* ANNE
catches him by the wrist.)

ANNE: No—
WILL: If I keep you now I lose myself. Don't you see?

(*She sees, bows to it, yes.*)

Make me that gift—
ANNE: No.
WILL: —of myself. Let me go.

(*A whisper.*)

Let me go—
ANNE: No—

(*But at last she releases his wrist; he snatches up
the sack, and backs away.*)

WILL: God forgive me.

(*He turns, and runs stumbling off.*

ANNE *bends over* SUSANNA's *head. And presently
the night commences to descend around them;
voices murmur, a few townspeople drift in, among*

them the townsman with the lute, softly singing—

> *—live but a fool to pine;*
> *'Twas I that beat the bush,*
> *The bird to others flew—*

and in the gathering darkness others wander on,
some passing, some halting to eye her curiously;
then nothing more is visible.)

END OF THE PLAY